Options Trading

The complete guide to Investing, Making a Profit and Passive Income For Your future Empire with These Simple Beginners' Strategies

By

Joseph Stone

Contents

Book One

Options Trading for Beginners

A simple Guide to investing and making profit with options trading in Few Weeks

By

Joseph Stone

Introduction

Options' trading is not for everyone, especially if you lack discipline in your trading. Furthermore, you will not be profitable unless you have a proper setup with an accuracy of at least 80%. Similarly, if you don't have proper money management in place, you'll almost certainly lose money when trading options. Furthermore, if you don't master the art of loss-cutting, you might end up losing a lot of money. Options' trading is not the field for you if you lack patience, can't control your greed, or can't stop averaging your losing position. Furthermore, if you are unable to stop overtrading and use ITM Options, you will be in serious trouble when trading options. On top of all of this, if you can't stop gambling and resist taking BTST and STBT trades, you might end up losing all of your investment. You can always make money trading options if you trade with discipline and have the right setup with an accuracy of at least 80%. Similarly, if you have proper money management in place and are skilled at cutting losses in small increments, you can successfully avoid huge losses in options trading. In options trading, your patience will always be the key to your success. So you don't have to be concerned about trading options if you have the patience to wait for the right opportunity and only trade 2–3 times per day. Furthermore, if you can control your greed and break your bad habit of averaging your position, you will always be able to make money trading options. If you don't overtrade and aren't afraid to use ITM options, you won't have any problems with options trading. If you let go of your gambling attitude and instead start trading with the right mindset and trading strategies, you can easily make money in options trading. You will always be a winner in options trading if you think about keeping your capital first by preventing risky trades like STBT or BTST. The riskiest tool is the option; if the trade goes against you, you could lose a lot of money. A trader's primary goal should be to conserve capital, with profit as a secondary goal. Option trading is worthwhile if it generates profits. You don't trade for the sake of making a few good trades. Similarly, you don't trade to see the green and red numbers on the monitor screen flicker. The value is derived from the outcomes. Without a doubt, if you believe in your trading ability and have faith in your trading strategy, you can become a millionaire through trading options. If you have the ability to maximize your winning trade and have the courage to quit a losing trade, then options trading will be a piece of cake for you. You do not have to be over aggressive, and must learn and practice to trade in your comfort zone while taking positions in options market

CHAPTER 1: What is Options Trading?

An option is a contract that allows (but does not obligate) an investor to buy or sell an underlying instrument such as a security, ETF, or index at a specific price over a specific time period. The options market, that trades contracts based on securities, is where you buy and sell options. A "call option" is one which allows you to buy shares at a later date, whereas a "put option" allows you to sell shares at a later date. Options, on the other hand, are not the same as stocks in that they do not constitute ownership in a company. And, while futures and options both use contracts, options are considered to be less risky because you can withdraw-or walk away from- an options contract at any time. The option's premium (price) is therefore a %age of the underlying asset or security. When a trader or investor buys or sells options, that particular investor or trader has the right to exercise the option at any time up until the expiration date; therefore, simply buying or selling an option does not imply that you must exercise it at the buy/sell point. Options are classified as derivative securities because of this system. This means that options price is derived from something else (in this case, from the value of assets like the market, securities or other basic instruments). As a result, options are frequently regarded as less risky than stocks (if used correctly). Why would an investor, on the other hand, use options? Basically, buying options is betting on stocks to go up, down, or to hedge a market trading position. The "strike price" is the price at which you promise to buy the underlying security via the option, and the "premium" is the fee you pay to purchase that option contract. When deciding on the strike price, you're betting on whether the asset (usually a stock) will rise or fall in value. The premium, which is a percentage of the asset's value, is the price you pay for that bet.

1.1 Options-Past and Present

Modern options contracts were instituted when the Chicago Board of Options Exchange (CBOE) was established, but it is believed that the fundamental concept of options contracts was established in Ancient Greece: possibly as long ago as in the mid-4th century BC. Since then, options have been present in different markets in one form or another, right up until the creation of the CBOE in 1973, when they were appropriately standardized for the first time and trading of options gained some credibility. In scope and sophistication, today's futures markets vary greatly from the barter systems that were first set up by the Japanese. Advances in technology have made trading options and futures more readily available to the average investor, as you might suspect. Most options and futures are electronically executed and pass through the Options Clearing Corporation (OCC), a clearing agency. Their global reach is a new feature of today's futures and options markets. Most big countries have vast markets and exchanges of futures on products ranging from weather, commodities, stocks, and now even returns from Hollywood films. The futures market has global breadth, just like the stock market. It is not without risk to globalize futures exchanges. Fundamentals and psychology of market turned down with significant intensity, as we saw during the meltdowns of last decade, mainly due to derivative protections. The results for the stock and futures markets might have been much worse had there been no government intervention.

What are Options?

Options are securities which grant the investor the option to purchase or sell an asset at a predetermined price, called the strike price, over a specified period of time, without any specific precondition. The amount of time may be as brief as a day, or as lengthy as a few years, depending on the form of contract available. There are only two forms of regular contracts with options: a call and a put. Trading options is simple to understand, as long as you learn certain important points. Investor portfolios are generally built with multiple asset classes. These could include stocks, bonds, ETFs and even mutual funds. Options are another asset class and offer many advantages that trading stocks and ETFs alone cannot possibly offer when used correctly. Like other asset classes, options can be purchased with an investment account. Options are powerful, because they can improve the portfolio of an individual. They do this by adding income, providing protection and even leverage. Depending on the case, there is typically a scenario of options tailored to the target of an investor. To limit downside losses, a popular example would be to use options as an efficient hedge against a falling stock market. Also, options can be used to generate recurring revenues. In addition, they are commonly used for gambling reasons, such as wagering on stock direction. Trading of options involves certain risks which the investor must be aware of before making a trade. Options involve risks and are not appropriate for everyone. Trading of options may be risky in nature and bear significant risk of failure.

- An option is a contract that gives the buyer the right, but not the obligation, to buy or sell (in the case of a call) the underlying asset at a specific price on or before a specific date.

- Traders use income, speculation and risk-hedging options.

- Options are also referred to as derivatives since they derive their value from the underlying assets.

- A stock option contract usually comprises 100 percent of the underlying stock, but options can be drawn up on some type of underlying properties, from debt to currency to product.

1.2 Types of Options

There are two options. It is important to note; the owner is not obliged to exercise his or her right to buy or sell for both types of option contracts. A brief description and roles of each is given below:

1.2.1 Call Option

A call option contract grants the owner the right to purchase 100 shares of a specified security within a specified time frame at a specified price. A call b provides you the right to buy a stock at a certain price on a certain date, with the expiration option. The call buyer will give a sum of money known as a premium for this right that the call seller will get. Not Like stocks that can live in perpetuity, after expiration an option will not exist, ending either worthlessly or with some cost.

Parts of Call Option

The following parts contain the major characteristics of an option:
Strike price

The price at which you will purchase the underlying stock
Premium

The cost of the option, for either the buyer or the seller
Expiration

When the option runs out and is settled

Call Option in action

Each option is considered a contract, and the underlying stock contains 100 securities in each deal. Exchanges quote options in terms of interest per unit, not the overall amount you have to pay to buy the deal. For example, on the exchange, an option might be offered at $0.75. And it would charge (100 shares x 1 contract x $0.75), or $75 to purchase one contract.

If the purchase price is over the strike cost at maturity, the call options are in the bank. The call owner may use the option, setting up cash at the strike cost to buy the stock. Or the owner can actually sell the right to another buyer at its good market price.

A call owner earns profit on less than the difference between the strike price and stock price the when the premium is paid. Suppose, for starters, that a dealer purchased a $0.50 call with a $20 strike price, and that supply is $23. The option valued $3 and the trader made a revenue of $2.50.

If the purchase price at maturity falls below the selling amount, otherwise the call is out of the market and expires useless. The call seller retains the option for any premium collected.

1.2.2 Put Option

A put option contract gives the owner the right to sell within a given time frame 100 shares of a specified security at a specified price. Each contract represents 100 shares, or the stock on which the option is based. Putting options enables traders to magnify downward market changes, transforming a slight price decline into a big benefit for the put buyer.

Components of Put Option

The following components contain the major characteristics of an option:
Strike price
A price at which you will sell the main stock
Premium
The cost of the option, for the buyer or the seller
Expiration
When the option runs out and is resolved
Put Option in action
For that privilege, the put buyer pays the put seller a premium per share. At expiry, if the price of the stock is lower than the price of the strike, the put value grows in money. The interest of the put in this case is

proportional to the strike price minus the selling price times 100, as each contract contains 100 securities. Unless the price of the stock is greater than the strike, the put is useless.

1.3 How can you trade Calls and Puts?

Four activities can be performed with options:
- Purchase Calls

- Sell calls

- Buy puts

- Sell puts

Buying stock provides a long position for you. Buying a call option will give you a potentially long position in the underlying stock. Short selling of a stock provides you with a short position. Selling a naked or uncovered call in the underlying stock gives you a potential short position. Buying a put option in the underlying stock gives you a potentially short position. Selling a put option gives you a theoretically long place in the stock underlying it. Those who purchase options are classified as investors and others who offer options are named options writers. Here's the big difference between holders and writers:
There is no requirement for call investors and put investors (buyers) to buy or sell. They are granted the opportunity to exercise their privileges. This reduces the chance of options owners to just paying the premium. However, call writers and put writers (sellers) are obliged to buy or sell if the option expires. This means a seller may need to make good on a purchase or sell pledge. It also means that sellers of options are subject to additional, and in certain situations infinite, threats. It ensures writers will risk a lot more than the quality of premium options.
Options Expiration & Liquidity
Also, options can be categorized according to their duration. Short-term options are options which usually terminate within one year. Long-term options with expirations longer than one year are known as shares where the holder hopes for a jump in price in the long-term. LEAPS are similar to standard solutions, they simply last longer. Also, options can be distinguished when their expiry date falls. Sets of options also expire regularly on a Monday, at month's end, or even hourly. Index and ETF choices also often sell expiries annually.

Options and Speculation
A speculator might think a stock's price will rise on the basis of a fundamental analysis or technical analysis. A speculator may purchase stock or purchase a call on stock option. Speculating with an incentive to call — rather than purchasing the stock directly — is appealing to certain traders because options have leverage. An out-of-the-money call option will pay just a few bucks, or just cents, relative to a $100 stock full price.
Options and Hedging
Hedging with options is intended to reduce risk at reasonable expense. Say you intend to buy inventories of equipment. Yet you do want losses to be minimal. You will reduce the downside exposure by utilizing put options, and reap all the upside in a cost-effective manner. Call options may be used by short sellers to reduce losses if incorrect-particularly during a short squeeze.

1.4 Options Trading and its benefits

Options provide more strategic (and economic) leeway to investors than they can get by just selling, buying, or shorting stocks. Traders can use portfolio loss protection options, snag a security for less than it manages to sell on the open market (or sell it for more), maximize the total returns on an existing or new position, and reduce the risk of speculative betting under all kinds of market conditions. Yes, in the pros vs. cons of options trading, there are a lot of positives. But there are inherent risks as well. Here are some things that should be considered by every prospective options trader.
You do not require large funds to initiate options' trading
An options' purchasing cost (the premium along with the trading commission) is comparatively much lower than what a trader would have to pay to buy securities directly. Traders pay less money to play in the same sandbox, but they will gain just as much (percentage-wise) if the trade goes their way.
Options are comparatively less risky as compared to other trading instruments
You are not required to follow through on the trade when you purchase a put or call option. If your assumptions are incorrect about the time frame and direction of the trajectory of a stock, your losses are limited to anything you paid for the contract as well as trading fees.
You are free to opt for different trading strategies

Before the expiry of an options contract, investors have the liberty to use various strategic moves, including:

- Use the option and purchase the shares to add to their portfolio

- Use the option, purchase the shares and then sell some or all of them

- Sell the "in the money" options contract to a different investor

- Has the option to recover some of the money incurred on an "out of the money" option. This can be done by selling the contract to another investor before its expiry

Options offer the trader to choose price
Option contracts allow investors to freeze the stock price at a specific amount of dollars (the strike price) for a specific period of time. Based on the type of option used, it ensures that investors will be able to purchase the stock at the strike price any time before the expiry of option contract.

1.5 Basics of Options' Pricing

The value of stock options is determined from their underlying shares' value and, depending on the results of the associated shares, the trading price for options can increase or decrease. With options, there are a variety of elements to understand.
The Strike Price

The strike price for an option is the rate at which, if the option is exercised, the underlying asset is purchased or sold. In the peculiar jargon of options, the relationship between the strike price and a stock's market price determines the following:

- Option is in-the-money

- Options is at-the-money

- Option is out-of-the-money

In-the-money
The strike price of an in-the-money call option is below the real market price. Example: At the $95 strike price for WXYZ, an investor buys a call

option that is already trading at $100. The investor's position is $5 in-the-money. The call option grants the investor the right to purchase the shares at $95. The strike price of an In-the-Money Put option is above the real market price. Example: At the WXYZ's $110 strike price, which is currently trading at $100, an investor buys a Put option. In-the-money is $10 for this investor position. The Put option grants the seller the right to sell equity at $110.

At the money

For both Put and Call options, the strike and the actual stock prices are the same.

Out-of-the-money

The strike price of an out-of-the-money call option is above the real market price. Example: At the strike price of $120 for ABCD, which is actually trading at $105, an investor buys an out-of-the-money call option. The position of this investor is $15 out-of-the-money. The strike price of an out-of-the-money put option is below the real market price. Example: At the $90 strike price of ABCD, which is currently priced at $105, an investor buys an out-of-the-money Put option. The position of that investor is $15 out-of-the- money.

The Premium

The premium is the price for an option that a customer pays to the seller. On purchasing, the premium is paid up front and is not reimbursable- even though the option is not applied. Premiums on a per-share basis are quoted. So, a $0.21 premium reflects a $21.00 per option contract ($0.21 x 100 shares) premium payment. There are many considerations that decide the amount of the premium-the prevailing stock price in comparison to the strike price (intrinsic value), the period of time before the offer expires (time value) and the price fluctuations of the commodity (volatility value).

Intrinsic value + Value of time + Value of volatility = option price

For example, at a strike price of $80, an investor buys a three-month call option for a volatile security that trades at $90.

Intrinsic Value = $10

Time value = because the call is 90 days away, the time value will be slightly applied to the price.

Volatility value = Because the underlying security is volatile, the volatility premium might be added.

Factors impacting options prices

Following factors have an impact on options prices:

The underlying equity price in relation to the strike price (intrinsic value)

The length of time until the option expires (time value)
How much the price fluctuates (volatility value)

Additional factors that have an impact on option prices

Additional facts that have an impact on options prices are:
The underlying equity's quality
The underlying equity's dividend rate
Prevailing market conditions
The underlying equity's supply and demand for options
The existing interest rates

Additional costs: Taxes and commissions

Investors that trade options, as in virtually any investment, must pay income taxes and also commissions to brokers on options trades. The net profit gain would be impacted by these costs.

1.6 Pricing Spreads in Options and Trading Strategies

A call spread relates to the purchasing of a call on a strike, and the selling of another call for a higher strike of the same expiry. An option strategy in which a call option is purchased is a call spread, and another less costly call option is sold. A put spread relates to purchasing a put on a strike, and selling another put on the same expiry's lower price. An option technique in which a put option is purchased is a put spread, and another less costly put option is sold. This transaction is less dangerous than an outright buy, since the call and put options have identical features, but it often provides less benefit. If you think that the underlying price will shift in a certain direction, and wish to reduce your original outlay if the forecast is wrong, these techniques are beneficial to try.

Advantages of Spreads

When you want to mitigate risk, spreads are useful for trading. Typically, spreads are traded by arbitragers to gain an edge on the transaction with close strikes, and then control the position. Position takes in trading premiums as the short option premium tends to cover the cost of the long option.

Call spreads buying considerations
Consider buying call spreads in the following situations:
If you are sure that the underlying security is destined to go up after which volatility will subside(e.g. a news event)
When you are sure that the underlying security is definitely going to edge up moderately
When you are sure that the underlying security's price will decline sharply, thus generating a sale of the underlying security
Consequently, the call spread will guard you against a petty upside move
Put spreads buying considerations
Consider buying put spreads in the following situations:
If you are sure that the underlying security is going to edge downward resulting in decrease in volatility (e.g. a news event)
If you are sure that the underlying security is going to depict decline in a limited range
If you are sure that the underlying security is going to fall sharply

Bull call spread

One long call along with a lower strike price plus one short call at a higher strike price is a bull call spread. The very underlying stock and the same expiry period are required for both calls. For a net debit (or net cost) and gains as the underlying stock increases in price, a bull call spread is built. Profit is impaired if the stock price increases above the short call strike price, and the possible loss is restricted if the stock price moves below the long call strike price (lower risk).

Bear Call Spread
A bear call spread, or a bear call credit spread, is a form of strategy of options which is used when an options trader believes the cost of the main stock to fall. By buying call options at a particular strike price although selling the same amount of calls at the same maturity date, but at a low strike cost, a bear call spread is established. Using this technique, the full profit to be made is equivalent to the credit earned while beginning the trade.
A short call spread is another name for a bear call spread. It is deemed as a strategy with limited-risk and limited-reward.

Calendar call spreads
You sell and purchase a call with the same strike price while running a calendar spread with calls, but the call you purchase would have a later date of expiry than the call you sell. As expiration approaches, you take advantage of accelerating time decay on the front-month call, also known as shorter-term call. You want to purchase back the shorter-term

call right before the front-month expiration for almost nothing. You will sell the back-month call and close your position at the same moment. Ideally, there would also be considerable time value for the back-month call.

Bear Put Spread

A bear put spread consists of a higher strike price for one long put and a lower strike price for one short put. Both puts have the same underlying stock and the same expiry date. For a net debit (or net cost) and earnings as the underlying stock decreases in price, a bear put spread is created. Profit is restricted if the stock price falls below the lower strike price of the short put strike), and if the stock price increases above the long put strike price (higher strike), the possible loss is limited.

Bull Put spread

A bull put spread consists of a higher strike price for a short put and a lower strike price for a long put. Both puts have the same underlying security and the same expiry date. For a net credit (or net sum received) and gains from either an increasing equity price or from time erosion or from both, a bull put spread is created. Potential benefit is restricted to the net premium earned less commissions and potential loss is reduced if the stock price drops below the long put strike price.

Calendar put spread

By purchasing one "longer-term" put and selling one "shorter-term" put with the similar strike cost, a long calendar spread with puts is established. Consider the following example. 100 Put is bought for two months (56 days to expiration) and 100 Put is sold for one month (28 days to expiration). For a net debit (net cost), this strategy is established and both the profit opportunity and the risk are minimal. If the stock price matches the strike price of the puts on the closing date of the short put, the maximum profit is obtained and the maximum risk is achieved if the stock price shifts sharply away from the strike price.

CHAPTER 2: Fundamentals of Options Trading

To better understand options trading, let's look at a simple example. Assume you're purchasing a stock for US$ 300. However, the broker informs you of an exciting offer: you can buy it now for US$ 300 or give a token amount of US$ 30 and reserve the right to buy it at US$ 300 in a month's time, even if the stock's value rises during that time. However, that small sum is non-refundable. You recognize that the stock has a good chance of crossing US$ 330, and thus you can at least break even. Because you only have to pay US$ 30 now, you can put the rest of the money towards something else for a month. You wait a month before checking the stock price. You now have the option of buying the stock from the broker or not, depending on the stock price. Of course, this is an oversimplification, but this is the essence of options trading. Options are derivatives, which means their price is derived from elsewhere, most commonly stocks, in the world of trading. An option's price is inextricably linked to the underlying stock's price.

2.1 How to buy a Call Option?

When the cost of the underlying asset rises to a price better than the strike price of the contract, the buyer of the option call seeks to benefit. The call option seller, on the other hand, expects the asset's price to fall, or at the very least never increase as high as the exercise price / strike value, before the option expires, in case the money taken for selling the option will be genuine incomprehensible profit. For example, imagine you've purchased an option on 100 stocks, with a $30 option to hit. Before your option runs out, the stock price increases from $28 to $40. You will then exercise the right to purchase 100 stock options at $30, granting you an instant $10 a share benefit. Your overall income will be 100 options, $10 for a share, minus the sales price you were charged for the option. If you had paid 200 dollars for the call option in this case, then your total income will be 800 dollars (100 shares x $10/share-$ 200 equals to $800).

Buying call options helps buyers to spend a small sum of money to theoretically profit from the rate increase in the underlying security, or to guard from the positional risks.

2.2 How to sell a Call Option?

Sellers of call options, also called writers, offer call options in the expectation that they may become useless by the expiry date. They earn money by pocketing the rates (prices) they have been paying. An income would be decreased, or possibly turn into a total loss, if the option holder performs the option profitably as the underlying security cost falls past the option strike point. The call options are offered in two ways:

Covered Call Option

If the call option seller holds the underlying stock, then a call option is covered. To Sell the call options on the underlying securities brings in extra gain, which would mitigate any anticipated market price decreases. The seller option is "covered" compared to a loss since if the buyer option exercises its option, the seller can provide the buyer with stock shares which he has already bought at a low price than the option's strike price. The seller's income in holding the underlying stock would be restricted to raising the stock to the strike price, but he will be shielded from any real loss.

Naked Call Option

A naked call option is one that is sold by an option seller who does not own the underlying stock. Because there is no limit on how higher the price of a stock can go and the owner of the option is not "protected" by holding the underlying stock against future losses, naked short selling of options is regarded exceedingly dangerous. When a call option holder practices his or her right, the bare option seller is compelled to buy the shares at the current market price and deliver the securities to the option holder. The gap between the current market price and the strike price reflects the seller's loss if the stock price surpasses the strike price of the call option. To compensate for any potential losses, most option sellers charge the full cost.

2.3 How to buy and sell a Put Option?

You can produce double-digit salary and returns by selling put options even in a bearish, flat, or overvalued market. For big returns on investment, you do not require a great bull market or rapid business growth. In the case of a market collapse, you may even grant your investments 10 per cent guarantee against downside. In other words, if the market falls by 25%, your equity positions are likely to fall by only 15%. You can also enter stock positions exactly at the price you want and keep the cost base low. You should try to purchase in a declining market to get a greater bargain instead of buying at presently available market rates. Like any device, there is a perfect period and place for selling put options and certain times it is not an optimal strategy. This is a sophisticated and best way of entering equity positions, when used correctly. To option sellers, the two most critical things are the bid and the strike. The strike is the price on which you agree to purchase the shares for if the option is used, and the bid is about the amount you can presume to earn on selling the option. If you sell an option with a strike price of 30 dollars less than the current stock price of 30.50 dollars, you will now receive $143 from the option buyer, and you will be obliged to purchase 100 shares of the company at $30 each if the buyer wishes, for an over-all of $3,000, at any time before the option expires in 3½ months. If the particular company's stock generally stays above $30 / share over the next 3½ months, the option buyer probably won't assign the shares to you, as When the market rate is already above $30 a share, there's no need for her to compel you to pay absolutely $30 a share. Her option will end worthlessly, you will keep your $143 premium, and your $3,000 in protected cash will be released for another option to be sold. Here is the calculated rate of return, if the right expires: $143 / $2,857 = 0.05 = 5%
After around 3.5 months, you made a return yield of 5 per cent on your early currency. This will be around 18 percent annual returns on your investment if you practice that for the remainder of the year a few of times. Compare this with the historical return of S&P 500 of around 9%. Compared to average stock returns, you're being charged a huge amount of money to only hang around and wait on for a market drop on a business you'd like to buy. On the contrary, if the stock dips to $29.50

per share, you still have to retain the 143 dollars premium, and the buyer option will appoint you to purchase the 100 shares for 30 dollars each. It means that your effective price base for buying those shares was just $28.57, which, as you wanted, is less than your target buy cost. You ended up purchasing them for $30 apiece, but you still got a $1.43 / share bonus up front, which covered some of the expense. The total cost structure is that for 100 securities you have to spend $28.57 / share, or $2.857. So instead, you hold 100 shares of a company already selling for $29.50 each. You purchased a wonderful business at a decent price and ideally you should still anticipate lots of growth in profits and bonuses over time.

CHAPTER 3: Getting Started in Option Trading

Options trading was once thought to be a practice that was best for financial professionals, but it has grown in popularity among individual investors over time. Options trading reached a daily average of more than twenty million contracts per day in 2018, a new high compared to previous years. Trading options can benefit new and beginning investors, and they can use measures to guard against risk as well as increase their profit potential. Trading options can add a lot of flexibility to your investment strategy when you consider volatility, time value and interest rates. You'll have to learn the language before you begin. Understanding what a strike price is and the difference between call and put options is crucial to fully comprehending what you're getting yourself into. You'll need a trading account with an options brokerage to begin trading options. After you've set up the account, you could start trading options with your broker, who will execute the trades for you. We have explained the basic concepts in the previous chapters. It's relatively easy to get started with options trading, despite the fact that it might sound complex and can include a wide range of strategic approaches. You'll need a broker, and you should compare fees as well as account minimums to find one that fits your budget and investment style. Then it's time to come up with an options trading strategy. Options trading strategies, like most investments, are dependent on your specific objectives and risk profile, and can range from simple to complex. It is time to acquaint yourself with certain prerequisites for options trading.

3.1 Open a Trading Account

You will be asked if you want to open a cash account or a margin account when you open a trading account with a brokerage firm.
Cash Account vs. Margin Account

The difference between a margin account and a cash account is that a margin account enables you to borrow funds from the brokerage by using your existing holdings (such as stocks and/or long-term options) as collateral. You can only use the cash in the account to pay for all of your stock and option trades if you have a cash account.
Minimum Deposit

A minimum deposit is usually required for opening a trading account. The amount required varies according to the type of account you're opening and the brokerage firm. To open a cash account, you only need a small deposit, whereas federal regulations demand a minimum deposit of $2000 for opening a margin-enabled account.
Online Brokerage vs. Offline Brokerage

Trading options effectively requires using an online brokerage account because there are lots of variables in an options trade compared to a stock trade. When you have to communicate too many details about a trade to the broker over the phone, you run the risk of miscommunication, which can be very costly. With today's advanced technology, online brokerages for options now provide highly intuitive user interfaces that make placing option trades online far easier than doing so over the phone. Furthermore, whilst a human broker can only deal with one client at a time, online brokerages can deal with thousands of orders at the same time. As a result, it's no matter of chance that the rise of option trading parallels the phenomenal advancement of internet technologies.

3.2 Things To Know As A Beginner

If you're thinking about trading options for generating profits, you may wonder if it's a decent time to start trading. Guidelines are available that you could always follow.

Be aware of minimum account required for trading options

To trade options, each online broker needs a different minimum balance. The mandatory minimum deposit for most brokerages is less than $1,000. Investors fill out a brief questionnaire inside their investment account to submit for options trading authorization. It is possible to get access to begin executing options directly afterwards.

Clear all debt

Get out of debt first. Pay off the car loans and credit card balances, explicitly. It's because of those loans, you're losing income anyway. Instances of' good debt' are known to be leases and student loans, while auto loans and credit card balances are perceived as instances of' bad debt.' The bottom line is that, before you start trading options, you must get out of bad debt.

Don't get stressed out while learning to trade options

You're also not fully in a spot to trade options even after you've eliminated the bad debt. You first have to know yourself. And if you believe you're ready and in the past you traded stocks, you still aren't done. Trading options are totally separate from trading securities. And before you trade options, you have to understand the stock market. However, you still need to learn quite a bit more. Start by studying the essentials. Understand the distinction between options for call and options for put. Know about expiration dates for contracts and strike prices. The trading of options is for persons who delve extensively into the data to assess the most advantageous trades. Traders who overlook certain stats are sometimes burnt.

Learning is the key to success

When it applies to options trading, you have never "arrived." There is always something that an expert trader will learn from you. Keep practicing also though you have trained yourself and mastered trading to the extent that you value your expertise as a trader. Strive to make yourself a greater trader every day.

Keep practicing

Before you allocate real capital, you need to do some practice trading. This is because, before doing the real thing, everybody wants to do some practice trading. When you invest in the capital markets, there are things you can learn. The quick way rather than the rough way is easier to learn such lessons. Fortunately, trading platforms are accessible that enable you to learn trading. Without losing some of your hard-earned assets, you can establish a pretend portfolio and begin trading stocks and options. And, as time progresses, you will see how the trades are successful. Take the time to assess what went wrong if you're not profitable, so that you can stop making such errors in the future.

Be aware of prerequisites for opening an Options trading account

Stock market options are limited-term contracts that offer owners the right to purchase or sell particular securities at a fixed date. In a broad variety of market techniques, the two forms of options — puts and calls — may be used to benefit from potential shifts in equity prices. To start purchasing and selling puts and calls, you must first register for account authorization. A trading account for options is a cash, margin or IRA stock brokerage account to which trading authorization for options has been applied. By completing a separate document, you incorporate options permission, plus a declaration of your trading background. The regulatory department of the broker checks the application for options and accepts your account with a degree of trading permission varying from one to five. What options strategies may be traded in the account are decided by the authorization levels. Novice investors can obtain one or two levels of authorization that enable strategies for lower-risk options.

You should be able to read a contract

Option contracts are purchased and sold using the online investment account's options trading screen. Under the options-chain link of a given stock, various put and call option choices can be identified. Choosing an option from the chain fills the trading screen with the specifics of a single option. You may then decide how many contracts you choose to purchase or sell and, if necessary, set a cap price. For a market order, the currently quoted "bid" price of an option is what you will pay to purchase. If you sell on the market, the "bid" price is what you would get. Each option contract is on an underlying stock of 100 securities, so one contract costs 100 times the quoted amount.

Should have sound knowledge of open and close orders

To start a trading position, options may be either bought or sold. Buying options grants you the right to purchase (call options) and/or sell (put options) the actual stock securities at a particular amount. If the customer uses his privileges under the options you have sold, trading options adds option premium earnings to the portfolio and the obligation to sell or purchase stock. You execute a buy-to-open or sell-to-open order to open an options position, depending on your approach. The order would be a sell-to-close or buy-to-close to close an options position in your portfolio.

Must have knowledge of Options Trading Platforms

To an online broker, there is no consumer more important than an options investor. Trades of options give brokers far larger operating profits than equity trades, and competitiveness is fierce for attracting these consumers as a consequence. This sort of business environment is perfect for consumers because product creativity and efficient prices come with fair competition. One can check for the following important characteristics when choosing a trading platform:

- Speed

- Low costs

- Options tools

The desktop application should have easy trading and intensive analysis. Option software should have personalized classification, real-time Greek streaming, and specialized position analysis for existing positions. It must give and show all the resources that an options trader would like in an efficient way. Some of them could be spread groupings, easy strategy screening, and risk / reward details that are simple to grasp. It must encourage customers to build custom rules and instantly roll up their current options positions. It should be outstanding for the amount of settings and depth of choice. Trading platforms can be built for both novice and experienced options traders. You as an investor should expect from your broker to include scanning, P&L analysis, risk analysis, and easy-order management.

The Broker's selection

Trading profitably allows you to use a brokerage company that aligns with your financial priorities, educational requirements and personal style. Choosing the right online stock broker that suits your needs, particularly for new investors, may mean the difference between an exciting new income stream and crushing disappointment.

Margins

In options dealing, "margin" often applies to the cash or assets needed to be deposited with the brokerage company by an option writer as collateral for the obligation of the writer to purchase or sell the underlying security or, in the case of cash-settled options, to compensate the balance of the cash payout if the option is assigned.

Margin call

In the case of an unfavorable market movement, margins are needed to guarantee that you will fulfill your future obligations. Margins are payable for option writers only, while buyers of options do not.

An Options margin call is where the broker needs extra cash or stocks to be given by a customer who has written Options. A failure to fulfill a margin call can result in closing of your Options positions.

How are Margins triggered

A margin call can be triggered for a score of factors, but the most common reasons are:

When a position moves against you, it consequently increases your potential obligation under the Options contract.

The exchange increases the margin requirement against your positions. The exchange reduces the collateral value allowed on your shares deposited as cover.

CHAPTER 4: Step-By-Step Guide To Gain From Options

It is time that you learn in a sequential manner about options' trading style and steps required to make money with options.

4.1 First Step: Find the correct setups

To begin, you must first identify an underlying asset on which to trade options. You shouldn't just pick any asset here. You should search for specific criteria and trade options that meet all of them. Following are the important factors to consider when selecting assets for options trading.

Liquidity

When trading options, liquidity is perhaps the most essential factor to consider. Liquidity refers to how easy or difficult it is to exit and enter positions in each asset. High liquid assets are those that have a large volume, tough Bid/Ask spreads, and are thus simple to exit and enter. If you prefer to trade an illiquid asset, you may have difficulty exiting and entering positions, and there is a risk of losing money. As a result, it's critical to concentrate on assets that are extremely liquid and have a high volume. You should consider more than just the underlying asset's liquidity. You should also consider the liquidity of the underlying asset's options. It can be achieved by looking at some options' volume, Bid/Ask prices, and open interest. In general, you should switch to indices, ETFs, and stocks that are heavily traded and well-known. Most of these renowned assets must be liquid, with liquid options. Simply avoid an asset that isn't liquid enough.

Implied Volatility (IV)

The implied volatility of an underlying asset is the next important factor to consider when choosing one to trade. The impact of implied volatility on option pricing can be significant. As a result, knowing whether IV is high or low is critical. IV Rank can be used to determine whether IV is currently high or low. It's crucial to choose assets with high-level implicit volatility when selling options. As a result, options will be more expensive, resulting in a higher premium for you as an option seller. When you are selling options, look for liquid assets with an IV Level of at least 50.

The Price

You may not trade options on all the assets depending on the size of your account. If an asset has a lot of costly options and your current account is insignificant, you should probably look for something else. However, different strategies can be used to modify your risk. Some assets have a limited number of options, which can be costly. So, look for an asset that has options that are appropriate for your account size.

Upcoming News / Events

In addition to the previously mentioned facets, you should keep an eye on the asset's upcoming events or news. This can help put the previous points into context. For instance, if a stock has future earnings, indicated volatility will almost certainly be high, as many stocks move significantly after earnings. Prevent assets with major upcoming events, such as earnings. These assets will most likely shift more than new assets, lowering your chances of profit. Also, stay away from assets with a future ex-dividend date, as this can have a significant impact on your chance of assignment and the price of the option.

4.2 Second step: Form a directional assumption

The underlying asset's directional assumption is formed in the second step. Is it more likely to go up, down, or sideward? This step will have an impact on the strategy you choose for the next step. You could use fundamentals or technical analysis to come up with a directional assumption. But to be honest, it doesn't really matter because we're trading with a maximum probability of success. It means that the price of the underlying asset could go against you, but you wouldn't lose money right away. You should be able to profit if the underlying asset does not move dramatically. Few (high probability option) traders believe that agreeing on a direction is continually a 50/50 bet. As a result, many traders prefer to trade neutral strategies rather than directional ones. Your directional assumption may be inspired by your present portfolio in the future. You shouldn't do a lot of technical analysis in this situation.

Simply choose whether you're bullish, bearish, or neutral on the underlying asset.

4.3 Third Step: Select a strategy

Finally, it's time to choose a trading strategy. Some of the preceding factors, such as the directional price, assumption, and accessibility of options, should influence this decision. Stocks are less versatile than options. Depending on your directional assumption, you would sell or purchase a stock in stock trading. Options trading, on the other hand, allow you to choose from and merge hundreds of various methods. However, for this trading style, you must concentrate solely on a limited option policy. Because you want to sell options rather than buy them, all these strategies will be generally short approaches. You can pick between defined or undefined probability strategies based on your risk profile. Only certain option trading strategies work with high probability option selling. There are a few key elements that make strategies successful for this style.

Overall Short

You should concentrate on trading overall quick strategies since you will be selling options.
Collecting Premium
Because you are selling something, you should collect a credit to start an overall quick option strategy.

Time Decay

A high-probability option seller, time should be on your side. To put it another way, when opening a new position, the option Greek Theta must be positive. This will enable you to profit from the passage of time.

Implied Volatility

To profit from a drop in implied volatility, the option Greek Vega must be negative. This is a critical point.

High Probability

When selling options, you should have a high chance of profit. Concentrate on setups with a high probability. Don't be too directional, and instead bet on large jumps in any other direction.

4.4 Fourth Step: Find the right option

After you've decided on a strategy, you'll need to decide on an expiry date, strike prices, and other details. This, too, is dependent on individual factors such as account size, risk tolerance, and time. However, as a rule, 45 days before expiration is a better time frame. According to research, the best way to profit from rising time decay is to wait 45 days before it expires. However, you won't always be able to start a position with a 45-day expiration date. It's best to stick to monthly expiration dates and avoid weekly options. Liquidity is the major excuse for this. Weekly options have a lot less open interest and volume than monthly options. When trading options, it's critical to keep your stakes low. Even with a high-powered option trading strategy, you won't always win. There will always be losing trades, and it is critical to keep them small. The only way to achieve this is to deal small amounts on each trade. Never put too much of your account's money into a single trade. It is strongly advised that you keep your chance to a maximum of 1-10 percent of your account per position.

4.5 Fifth Step: Choose the correct price

There is one final thing to ponder before sending out the order, and it is the price. Always make sure you have sufficient balance to establish the trade worthwhile. You must also consider commissions if you have an insufficient amount. The trade is probably not worth if you just get $20 in premium and must pay 7 dollars in commissions. At least $50 must be brought in. You must also consider your reward / risk ratio. Because of the high likelihood of profit, this may not be the good option. Frequently, your maximum risk outweighs your maximum reward. But that's fine if your chances aren't too slim. For instance, you should not risk $1000 in order to get $100 with a 40% chance of profit. Though, take the risk of $250 in order to get $100 with a 75% return is perfectly acceptable. Furthermore, limit orders should always be used. This will result in good pricing and a higher perceived value. Your order can be filled quicker but at a lower price if you use a market order. You can set your own price when you use limit orders. You can frequently get filled at a medium price in highly liquid assets. If you do this, every trade will get you a few dollars. If you add up to hundreds or thousands of dollars, this can be a significant sum of money.

4.6 Sixth Step: Make money with options

You've now completed the trade. This step primarily entails expecting for the sold option(s) to reduce their cost so that you can repurchase them for a lower price than you originally paid. It is suggested that profits be taken at 50% of the maximum profit. This will rise your profit potential while also reducing the time spent on each trade. Getting profits soon will let you to place new trades more rapidly. You could computerize this process by placing a Good Till Cancel (GTC) order at 50% of your maximum profit just after you open your positions. Here's an example of what this could look like:

You get a $1.5 credit for filling a position (as a standard option contract operates 100 shares of stock). You can then continue by sending a $0.75 GTC debit order. The GTC order should be filled as soon as the position drops to around $0.75, and you will be automatically exited.

There are a few management options available if a situation doesn't work out as scheduled. Again, the management options are determined by the strategy you select. Because your risk isn't capped, undefined risk strategies should be handled more than defined risk strategies. Cutting losses at a certain point is a way to control the risk of undefined risk strategies. Another option is to apply the strategy to a credit with a later expiration phase. This can be repeated many times. Because you have a limited downside, handling defined risk strategies isn't as important. This maximum loss should be acceptable if you maintained your position size small enough. There are, however, a few approaches to adjusting defined risk strategies. It's critical not to abandon losing positions too quickly. This may appear to be unrealistic, but it isn't. It is always possible to turn a losing position into a successful one. It will be a guaranteed loss if you get it off at a loss. So, if the loss isn't too large and there's still time before the expiration date, you must try to grip on to losing trades. One more reason why small position sizes are essential is because of this. You will miss out on many potential winners if you must cut losses as soon as a position goes against you. Before the expiration date, several winning option positions are red. You shouldn't, however, keep to obvious losing positions. If you only have a short amount of time left or if a position is going against you then you must take the loss. Losing positions, especially those with less time left, must be rolled out or cleared. Due to assignment risk, this is the case. The risk of being assigned is known as assignment risk. Assignments are made only to short ITM option holders in the final week before expiration. Even with two days to go, a far ITM option isn't assured to be assigned.

4.7 Seventh Step: Start all over again

This is, without a doubt, one of the most crucial steps. If you want to make money with options, you must repeat the similar procedure repeatedly. We'll use an example to demonstrate why it's important to repeat this process:

A coin tossing game is used as an example. The game's rules are in which you toss a coin and if it come heads, you get $1; if it come tails, you lose $1. It's a 50/50 chance. You will be 1 dollar up or 1 dollar down if you toss the coin once. You must have gained 5 times, lost five times or anything in between if you tossed the coin five times. If you tossed the coin ten times, the result would be similar. However, if you toss the coin thousand times, you will almost certainly be at or near breakeven.

We can apply the same concept to our trading. The genuine outcome may differ from the probable outcome if we place 1, 2, or more small trades with a 70% chance of profit. Even if 2 trades have a 70% chance of profiting, they could very well end up being failures. However, if we place 200 trades with a 70% chance of profiting, it is highly not likely that all of them will lose. The more trades we make, the closer we move to our desired result. It is critical that you comprehend this. As a result, it's critical to boost the number of events as much as possible. This does not imply that you should place many trades at the same time. It simply suggests that you must approach this strategy with a long-term mindset. The numbers will eventually work themselves out. All you have to do now is stick with it long enough.

CHAPTER 5: Beginners Common Mistakes

When trading options, you can profit whether the stock price goes up or down or sideways. With a small cash outlay, you could use option strategies to minimize losses, preserve gains as well as handle large portions of stock. When trading options, you could also lose more than the full amount you spent in a small amount of time. That's why it's crucial to proceed cautiously. Even the most experienced traders can make a mistake and lose money. Beginners frequently make the following mistakes.

Buying Out-of-the-Money (OTM) Call Options

One of the most difficult ways to make consistent money in option trading is to buy OTM calls outright. Because they are inexpensive, OTM call options appeal to new option traders. Buying a cheap call option and seeing if you can pick a winner seems like a good place to start. Buying calls may appear safe because it follows the same pattern as buying low and selling high as an equity trader. However, if you only use this strategy, you risk losing money on a regular basis.

Misunderstanding of leverage

Most beginners take advantage of the leverage factor that option contracts provide, unaware of the risk they are taking. They are frequently attracted to buying short-term calls. For new option traders, a general rule is to start with one option if you normally trade 100 share lots. If you usually trade 300 share lots, you might be able to get three contracts. This is a good starting point for a test amount. If you don't succeed in these sizes, you're unlikely to succeed in larger trades.

Absence of exit plan

It's probably something you've heard a thousand times before. It's critical to keep your emotions in check while trading options, just as it is when trading stocks. This does not imply that you must swallow your fears in a superhuman manner. It's much easier than that: make a work schedule and adhere to it. Even when things seem to be going well, you should have a backup plan. Choose an upside and a downside exit point, as well as the timeframes for each exit, well ahead of time. What if you leave some upside on the table by leaving too soon? This is a common trader's concern. The best counter-argument is this: What if you could consistently make a profit, reduce your losses, and get a better night's sleep? Make a plan for how you'll get out of this situation. An exit strategy is essential whether you're buying or selling options. It assists you in developing more successful trading patterns. It also helps you to keep your worries in check. Ascertain an upside exit strategy and a worst-case scenario on the downside that you are willing to accept. Liquidate your position and take the profits if you achieve your upside targets. If you hit your downside stop-loss, you should exit the trade once again. Don't put yourself in any more danger by betting that the option price will rise. The temptation to go against this advice will almost certainly be strong at times. It's not a good idea. You must devise a strategy and then stick to it. Far too many traders devise a strategy and then abandon it as soon as the trade is executed in able to pursue their emotions.

Failure to adopt new strategies

Many option traders claim they would never buy or sell out-of-the-money or in-the-money options respectively. These absolutes seem ridiculous until you're in the middle of a losing trade. Keep an open mind when it comes to developing new option trading strategies. Remember that options are derivatives. This means that their prices do not move in the same way as the underlying stock or even have the same properties. Time decay, whether beneficial or detrimental to the position, must always be incorporated into your plans. You have to decide to close the trade, reduce your losses or look for a new opportunity that makes more sense right now. Options can provide a lot of leverage for a small amount of money, but they can also blow up just as swiftly as any other position if you dig too deep. Accept a small loss in exchange for a chance to avoid a disaster later.

Trading Options that are not liquid

Liquidity refers to a trader's ability to buy or sell something quickly without causing a significant price change. A liquid market is one where buyers and sellers are always ready to buy and sell. Another way to look at it is as follows: The likelihood that the forthcoming trade would be executed at the same price as the previous one is referred to as liquidity. For a simple reason, stock markets are much more liquid than option markets. Option traders might just have dozens of option contracts to choose from, whereas stock traders may only trade one stock. If the stock is extremely illiquid, the options on it are likely to be even less active. The bid as well as ask price for the options will usually have a large spread as a result of this. Trading illiquid options raises the cost of doing business, which is already higher than stock trading costs on a percentage basis. Don't put too much pressure on yourself. Make sure the open interest is at least 40 times the number of contacts you want to trade if you're trading options.

Waiting too long to buy back short options

Traders frequently wait far too long to buy back the options they've sold. There are also plenty of reasons for this. Consider the following scenario:

- You are adamant about not paying the commission.

- You're betting that the contract will be worthless when it expires.

- You want to squeeze out a little more profit from the trade.

Recognize when it's time to repurchase your short options. If the short option becomes far out of the money and you can profitably buy it back, do so. Don't be a miser. Here's a good rule of thumb: if you could somehow keep 80% or more of the profit from the option sale, you should consider buying it back. Otherwise, it's a foregone conclusion. Because you waited too long, a short option will bite you one of these days.

Failure to factor in upcoming events

Although not all market events can be predicted, there are two key activities to keep track of whilst trading options. For example, if you've sold calls and a dividend is approaching, your chances of being assigned early are higher if the option is already in the money. This is particularly true if a sizable dividend is expected. Because option holders do not have a right to a dividend, this is the case. The option trader must exercise the option as well as purchase the underlying stock in order to collect. Make sure to take into account upcoming events. You must, for example, be aware of the ex-dividend date. Also, unless you're willing to take a higher risk of assignment, avoid selling options contracts with pending dividends. Investing during earnings season usually means dealing with higher volatility in the underlying stock – and paying a premium for the option. If you want to buy an option during earnings season, you can create a spread by buying one option and selling another.

Legging into Spreads

Most novice options traders attempt to "leg into" a spread by purchasing one option first and then selling the other. They're attempting to reduce the price by a few pennies. It simply isn't worth taking the chance. If you'd like to trade a spread, don't "leg in." Spreads can be traded as a single trade. Don't take on unnecessary market risk. Always treat a spread as if it were a single trade. Don't get caught up in the details of timing. You want to enter the trade as soon as the market begins to fall.

Not knowing what to do when assigned

If you sell options, just keep in mind that you could be assigned before the expiration date if you sell them early. Many new option traders do not consider assignment as a probability until it occurs to them. Early assignment is one of those irrational and highly emotional market events. When it happens, it usually has no rhyme or reason. It's unavoidable. Even when the market indicates that it is a less-than-successful strategy. Plan ahead of time what you'll do if you're given a task. The best way to avoid an early assignment is to think about it ahead of time. Otherwise, it may lead to rash, spur-of-the-moment decisions that are less than rational.

Ignoring index options for neutral trades

Individual stocks have a high degree of volatility. For example, if a company experiences a major unanticipated news event, the stock may remain extremely bearish for a few days. Even significant turmoil in a major company that is part of the S&P 500, on the other hand, is unlikely to cause the index to fluctuate significantly. Index-based trading options can protect you from the massive swings that single news items can cause in individual stocks. Consider neutral trades on major indices to reduce the unpredictability of market news. Consider trading strategies such as short spreads (also known as credit spreads) on indexes, which can be profitable when the market is in sideways phase. In comparison to other strategies, index moves are less dramatic and far less likely to be influenced by the media.

CHAPTER 6: Advanced Trading Strategies

The good news is that with options, traders of all skill levels can learn how to trade the market. Options trading techniques typically utilize momentum metrics such as the Relative Strength Index (RSI) to warn them when market moves are overdone, either upside-down or downside-up, and are primed for reversal in the opposite direction. Also, traders tend to stay longer in a trade. It will make them better off to operate overnight as part of a swing trading plan, as acquired option positions have reduced downside danger. Option traders use a variety of options strategies which include buying and/or selling one or more options to take either directional or market-neutral views of the underlying asset market. These often usually use diagrams called option compensation or reward profiles to provide a quick understanding of whether the option plan would pay out with a variety of underlying market prices, including the one seen below, on the expiry date.

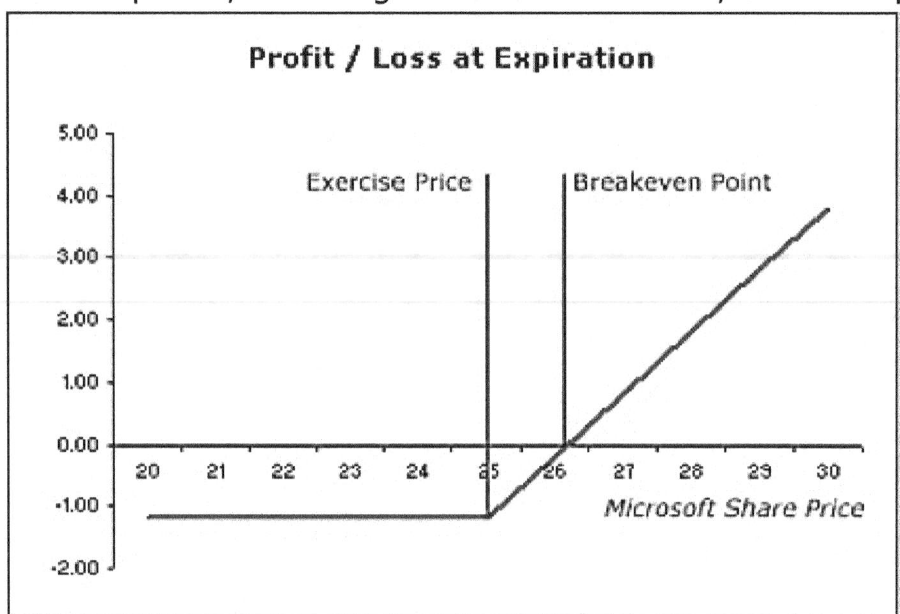

The blue line in that graph indicates how if the demand hits the breakeven stage, the option price begins making a profit at expiration. The position can also show a profit before expiry, however, if you can sell the option at a price higher than the purchase price. This is generally the goal when swinging trading the options. Fortunately, you can easily learn how to trade options to implement your market view for a directional trading strategy such as swing trading. The instructions below illustrate how to use a basic option strategy to swing trade in almost every financial asset sector where options are readily accessible, such as purchasing a call or put option.

Choose an asset

The first phase in swing trading with options is to pick an underlying commodity for trade that you have established as an incentive to sell. Swing traders would also track different equity markets in order to provide a better probability of having a successful trading setup. In picking an asset, search for equity price that is prone to a downturn as defined by a measure of momentum, such as the RSI. A specific measure is a range-bound oscillator that indicates an overbought position when its value is over 70 or oversold position when its value is below 30.

See when RSI moves above 70 and buy when it goes below 30

When you like any more accurate swing trading indications from the RSI, you should wait before you see something occurring called price-RSI variance, which implies that the market price rises briskly, such as reaching a new peak, but the RSI does not. That's an even stronger swing trading warning that an impending recession is coming to the market.

Select the right direction

Call Option   Put Option

For example, once you've identified a market and used your preferred form of market analysis, whether technical and/or fundamental, to find a trading opportunity with a good risk / reward ratio of 2 or more to 1, then you might feel comfortable using call and/or put options to take a directional market view of the underlying asset. For example, if you think the market is going to rise, you would use a call option to go long in the market with limited downside risk and unlimited upside potential for the underlying market you want to trade.

Alternatively, if your view was that the market would fall, instead you would buy a put option, again with limited risk of downside and unlimited potential for upside. The payoff profiles below shown for long call and put options at expiry shows how your losses are limited to the premium paid if your directional view turns out to be wrong. In addition, potential profits on an option position are unlimited and begin to accumulate past the breakeven point where the gains on the position exceed the bonus paid.

Choose the strike price

An option's strike price aids in determining its price. Generally speaking, the more attractive an option's strike price is in relation to the prevailing market price for the underlying asset, the more it will cost. Also, the longer time frame a particular strike price option has until expiry, the more it will be expensive. When strike rates are higher than the prevalent sector, it is assumed that they are either "in the pocket" or ITM. An option with an ITM strike price also has "intrinsic value," corresponding to the difference between the prevailing market price (for the delivery date of the option) and the strike price. When the strike price of an option is right on the prevailing market, it is "at the money" or ATM, and when it is "out of the money," or OTM, at a level worse than the prevailing market. There is no inherent interest on both the ATM and OTM products. Many swing traders are trying to take advantage of reasonably short-term price fluctuations in a sector, and they are likely to choose an OTM opportunity as they expect ITM to go fairly fast thus enabling them to sell it back. This is because options also have time value as well as intrinsic value and as time progresses towards expiration, the time value declines increasingly. This encourages a swing trader to sell back any option that they bought when a respectable profit presents itself at the first opportunity.

Select expiration date

Choosing an expiry date would represent in part how long you believe it would take the underlying market to achieve your target price. Generally speaking, you'll want to choose a shorter-term option if you think the transfer would be fast or a longer-term option, especially if you think it could take more time. For a swing trader, you simply don't want to have an option that expires so early because it could end up being useless at expiration. At the other side, owing to the comparatively high cost, you do not want to purchase an option with an expiry date so long in the future.

Decide about the entry time

Timing of trading entries is usually done using technical analysis. Since swing traders deal both with patterns and with adjustments to such patterns, they first need to recognize, if any, the dominant pattern in the commodity they are looking at. Swing traders would look for a corrective pullback while trading with the trend to create a position in trend direction. If the pullback seems to be losing steam, as shown by an RSI level in over-bought or over-sold range, preferably indicating price deviation, they will believe the time to enter the market is ripe.

Execute the trade

When the time has come for the trade, it's time to proceed according to the trading schedule. For example, if the overall trend is higher, you could buy OTM call option, or an OTM put option if the market is downward. It's always crucial to note that the way you deal is just as critical as the point at which you sell, so make sure you pick the best broker as your business partner. Transaction costs can really add up over time, including handling spreads and fees, if you trade frequently as a swing trader.

Manage the position

You run the risk of failure after you have conducted a trade and have a choice, but because you bought an option, the liability would be restricted to the price you paid for it. You may always need to track the underlying demand to better handle the option trade. If you purchase an OTM share, you will decide to sell it until the underlying market hits the price of the strike and it is ATM. If the time value rises, that would also result in the option picking up extra prime. Competing with potential gains will be the time decay occurring for every full day an option approaches its expiry date. This suggests that at the earliest moment possible you'll want to sell back the option position to prevent making a deal centered on a perception that was directionally sound risk value due to premature deterioration over time. If the market still seems like your trade would finally pan out, but the short-term change you planned to capitalize on has failed to materialize will allow it more time to come to fruition.

It may be achieved by conducting a calendar spread or roll-out swap that includes selling back your own near-term option and purchasing a longer-term option at the same strike price. This prevents you from taking losses as their expiration approaches because of the sharply increasing time decay on near-money options.

Married Put

An investor purchases an asset in a married put strategy and at the same time purchases put options on an equal amount of securities. The buyer of the put option is entitled to sell the stock at the strike price, and the value of each contract is 100 shares. When keeping a stock, an investor can opt to use this strategy as a way to minimize their downside risk. For instance, suppose an investor buys 100 stock shares and simultaneously buys one put option. In the case of a significant shift in the market price, this approach could be beneficial to this investor since they are shielded from the downside. Around the same moment, if the asset rises in value, the investor will be able to participate in any possibility of upside. The main drawback to this approach is that the investor sacrifices the balance of the premium charged on the put option if the stock does not decrease in value.

Long Butterfly

Butterfly spread options are made up of 2 vertical spreads with a similar strike price. In other terms, an opening position where options (either calls or puts) are acquired (or sold) at 3 separate strike rates includes butterfly options. The method in which these options are produced renders the butterfly a position of both limited loses and limited benefits. It is possible to build the Long Butterfly spread option using either all call options or all put options. A Long Butterfly formed using call options would work like one generated using put options due to put-call parity. In other terms, it doesn't really matter if you make your Long Butterfly using calls or puts.

Short Iron Condor Strategy

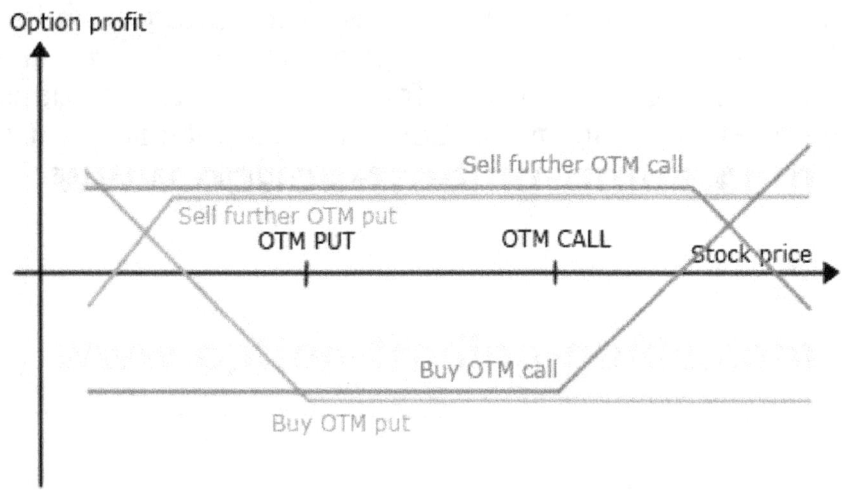

An advanced option trading technique that utilizes a mixture of two vertical spreads is the Iron Condor strategy. At strike prices that are greater than the current price of the underlying stock, a call spread is opened and a put spread is opened at strike prices which are lower than the current price. For volatile stocks, the Short Iron Condor technique is used. It is created by opening up a bullish out-of-the-money (OTM) call spread and a bearish out-of-the-money (OTM) put spread. You purchase an OTM call and you sell an extra OTM call. Then you purchase an OTM put then sell an OTM put, which is an extra OTM. This causes a scenario of debit spread, whereby when you open the position, you need to compensate the difference in premiums.

Long Iron Butterfly Options

The technique of the Iron Butterfly options is an advanced option strategy that uses 2 vertical spreads (1 call spread and 1 put spread) to build a position that is beneficial when you anticipate low volatility, or when you require great volatility but are unaware of the direction. The Iron Butterfly is close to the strategies of the Butterfly and Iron Condor, as the name suggests. It has the same profile for profit and risk as the Butterfly, but uses a mix of option spreads similar to the Iron Condor. The most widely used variant of the Iron Butterfly is Long Iron Butterfly options. They are ideal for stocks that would not change significantly (low volatility).

Conclusion

You are not forced to buy or sell while trading options. You actually have the right to trade two kinds of stock options instead: puts and calls. Participants in new options are enthusiastic about the advantages participants earn and make errors. There are certain errors that you must avoid during options trading like starting too big, using only one strategy, setting an illogical expiration date, purchasing out-of-the-money options and increasing the trades for making up losses. New option traders end up exacerbating their risk. Close failed trades instead of attempting to solve problems that have already damaged you and your money. When you understand when to close trades, you move a step closer to transitioning from a novice to a good option investor. A perfect way is to take a time-out and rest your minds from trading. Taking a break is going to really ideally place things in order. Understand, you're not going to lose much in a couple of hours, which is time to calm off. After all, a number of wonderful prospects are always waiting for you, just losing one or two carry no meanings and shall have no impact on your performance. It's better to live with the heat of passion than to risk all the capital. You just have to learn start trading with a cold head and enjoy your trades in the options market.

Book Two

Options Trading Crash Course

The Complete Crash Course To Learn How Investing And Making Money Online with Trading Options in 7 Days or Less!

By
Joseph Stone

Introduction

It's all about customization when it comes to investing with options. The stakes can be high, but so can be the risk, and you have many options. However, getting started is difficult, and costly mistakes can be made. Options trading is primarily aimed at the do-it-yourself investor. Option traders stand typically self-guided investors, which means they do not work with some financial advisor for managing the options trading profiles. You have complete control over your trading decisions and transactions as a do-it-yourself (D.I.Y.) investor. However, this does not imply that you are alone. There are numerous online communities where traders can discuss the current market outlook and option trading strategies. Most newcomers begin with stock options. Stock options, also known as equities options, are a type of option that is based on equities. Stock options are listed in the form of a quote on exchanges like the NYSE. Before you decide, it's critical to understand the specifics of stock options quotes, such as the cost and expiration date. A stock options quote is a compact form of detailed information. You can quickly understand important details of the option contract, such as the type, cost, and expiration date, once you understand what each segment represents. Contracts that give the owner the right to buy or sell an asset at a set price for a set period are known as options. Depending on the type of options contract, that period could be as short as a day or if a couple of years. Fortunately, standard option contracts are limited to only two types: call and put. Options can be used in various ways, including to speculate or mitigate risk, and they can be traded on a variety of underlying securities. Equities, indexes, and exchange-traded funds (ETFs) are the most common underlying securities (Exchange Traded Funds). There are several distinctions between index-based options and those depending on equities & ETFs. Before you begin trading, it's critical to understand the differences. As you will read this book, you will educate yourself on various aspects of options and options trading.

CHAPTER 1: Types of Investments

The premise behind all investment decisions is to generate money smartly and efficiently while keeping the risk factors to the minimum. As a prudent investor, you must select the best investment opportunity from the available options. You, being the investor, will be guided in your quest by researching for answers to different critical questions such as:

- What investment option offers the most secure return concerning Investment Time?

- Where is that particular investment option currently in its Business Cycle?

- When is the best time for committing the Investment Amount?

Prices do not move in a straight line, and the price activity is shaped by scores of factors stemming from changes in political and industrial policies to frequent shifts in international business supply and demand factors. This standard operating procedure is usually also followed in the Forex, Stock and Option Markets, with another crucial factor that attempts to seek and investigate the reasons behind such an investment decision. Succinctly, an investment decision revolves around the three W's.

1.1 What to Buy or Trade

Once you have arrived at an investment or trading decision, the next rational step is to set off a comparative analysis of different available investment options based on their liquidity. Liquidity is an attribute of an investment or trading option that makes it easily accessible during the buying and selling process. This first step will assist you in unraveling the best-performing investment or trading option based on its past and current performance.

1.2 Why Buy or Trade

The ensuing step should be to perform a threadbare analysis of investment options based on earning potential, market competitiveness versus exclusivity, price behavior etc.

1.3 When to Buy or Trade

Finally, a decision must be made on the investment time. Prices move in a wave-like pattern. This wave-like pattern owes its formation to the crest and troughs that appear on a graph due to respective highs and lows attained during a particular period. These highs and lows are materialized because of the respective bullish and bearish spells in the stocks and commodities. This is because all business cycles follow a cyclical movement of Growth (Expansion), Peak (Top), Decline (Contraction), Recession (Trough) and then back to Expansion. Commit your investment to an astronomically performing stock or commodity at the peak of the business cycle. You should be ready to be flushed out from the market bare-handed as peaks do not remain intact for a long time and stun the investors by the sharp downturn. Thus, the timing of investment is the most critical factor which must be worked out astutely. An investment or trading decision, no matter how smart, could result in the wiping of funds if not exquisitely timed.

1.4. Long-term vs. Short-term Investments

When devising an investment strategy, you must consider both long- and short-term objectives and select investments that reflect your goals. Finding the right balance is crucial to building a portfolio that works for you.

1.4.1 When should you choose long-term over short-term investments?

Long-term investments are those that you expect to keep for a long period. Long-term investments are assets such as stocks and real estate that you intend to hold for a long time. They allow you to grow your portfolio because you know you won't need the money for a long time.

1.4.2 Your retirement is more than 20 years away

If you're more than two decades away from retirement, there's still a long way to go before you stop working. Long-term investments, such as stocks, are a good asset class to build wealth over decades because they require time to grow.

1.4.3 You need a plan for seven to 10 years in the future

Another thing to think about is your timeline. Low- and medium-risk portfolios are common in financial plans for the next seven years.

However, when you get in the 7-10 years range, you will believe in riskier assets. In general, long-term investments such as stocks can be used for the money you won't need for a longer period. When you need money, dividend stocks are a good option for medium-term goals because they pay out regularly and can grow.

1.4.4 You want protection from inflation

Long-term investments may also be preferable if you want to beat inflation or be protected from it. Long-term investments, such as stocks, are often regarded as less safe than other assets, but they offer a higher potential rate of return over time, giving you a better chance of preserving your purchasing power.

1.4.5 When should you choose short-term over long-term investments?

Short-term investments are those that you intend to use to achieve financial objectives in a short period. Rather than building your portfolio, you may require the funds to provide a steady source of income. Bonds, cash, and annuities are examples of short-term investments. There are some circumstances in which short-term investments make sense.

1.4.6 When you need money soon

Short-term investments may make sense when saving for shorter-term goals, such as a down payment on a home. Specific deposit accounts, e.g., can offer a fixed rate of return while also allowing you to pull out funds whenever you want. You can put your cash into the money market short-term bonds or mutual funds and expect to be able to access it for a short-term goal without fear of a loss in the market.

1.4.7 You are looking for perpetual income

Short-term investments are frequently linked to a steady income. When you know, you'll need consistent income, investing in high-rated bonds and other assets can help. While the return isn't as high as it could be with some stocks, you have a better chance of dependable income.

CHAPTER 2: Trading and Different between Forex, Stocks and Options

Trading refers to exchanging one object for another. When we talk about financial market trading, it's the same principle. Talk to the one who is selling stock. What they do is purchase stock or a small part of a company. If the value of those shares' increases, they gain money by selling them at a higher price again. It is merchandising. You purchase it for one price and then offer it for another again — ideally at a better price, creating a profit and vice versa. But why would the shares be worth buying? The answer is simple as the price is subject to change with the changes in supply and demand. The more there's demand for something, the more people willing to pay for it. If a business reports some impressive results and pays out nice dividends, more investors tend to purchase the company's stock. The growing competition would contribute to price rise in certain securities. Trading is about purchasing and selling for benefit in the short term. It places great emphasis on the prices.

Traders take a position in the market daily, weekly, or intraday basis intending to make short-term profits. These often concentrate on the technological aspects of a financial device rather than its long-term prospects. Traders are mainly involved in exploring the market's short-term trend and recent and rapid stock changes to leverage on it and achieve short-term profits. Timing is important in business. Traders utilize price charts to evaluate rates and price trends daily, weekly, or minute-to-minute to decipher the expected market path. Alternatively, the funds are participating in the business with a long-term perspective. They speak in terms of years and usually hold positions for over a year. Investors look for stock prospects for long-term development or profitability, but traders also take advantage of significant market demand swings that occur because of minor or large political incidents or economic news.

2.1 Trading And Different Types

Technical traders can select from five main types of trading methods. It is very important to master one trading style, but the trader also needs to be skilful in others.

Scalping

This type of day trading includes the fast and repetitive purchasing and selling within seconds or minutes of a wide quantity of stocks. Scalping is a style of trade that specializes in profiting from small changes in prices. It needs a trader to have a clear exit plan since one major failure might erase the many minor profits that the trader managed to achieve. Scalping is based on the premise that the bulk of stocks enter the first step of a trend. Yet, there is confusion on where it goes from here. Some stocks cease to progress after the initial point, while others proceed. Without making them evaporate, a scalper plans to collect as many minor gains, as necessary. It is the reverse of the mentality of "let the earnings run," which seeks to maximize successful trade results by increasing winning transactions. By raising the number of winners and reducing the value of the gains, scalping produces efficiency. A good scalper should have a significantly higher ratio of winning trades than losing ones, thus retaining gains approximately comparable to or marginally greater than losses. Traders following this technique will place ten to a few hundred orders in a single day with the hope and belief that minor changes in equity markets are simpler to spot than large ones. A short-term market position reduces the risk of running into an adverse scalping case. Scalping can be implemented as a main or supplemental trading form.

Day Trading

Day trading can be a very lucrative career if you are doing it properly. However, it can also be a little challenging for novices — especially for those who are not completely equipped for a well-planned approach.

Only the most experienced day traders should be likely to encounter rough times and suffer losses. Day trading is defined as buying and selling a security within one business day. It may occur in any marketplace, but it is most common in foreign exchange (Forex) and capital markets. Day traders tend to be well-educated and well-funded. To profit on minor market swings in extremely volatile securities or currencies, they utilize large levels of leverage and short-term trading tactics. Day traders are attuned to developments that affect stock fluctuations in the short term. News-trading is a popular technique. Scheduled announcements are subject to market expectations and market psychology, such as economic statistics, corporate earnings, or interest rates. Markets react once those expectations aren't exceeded or met, usually with important, rapid movements that may benefit the day traders. Day traders use various intraday techniques. These strategies cover:

Trading in a sideways market
It focuses on buying near support and selling around resistance levels.

Trading based on news
This typically takes advantage of trading opportunities around news events due to the increased volatility.
High-frequency trading (H.F.T.)
It includes strategies using sophisticated algorithms to exploit market inefficiencies in the small or short-term.
Trading based on momentum
Momentum trading is a strategy whereby traders buy and sell depending on the severity of recent market patterns. In financial markets, momentum is determined by factors such as trading volume and corresponding price rate changes. Momentum traders assume that a rapidly rising security price in a specific direction would tend to shift in that direction before the trend loses power. Traders buy stocks with strong trends in price performance and then sell stocks whose prices do not perform well. Momentum trading can be divided into two categories:

Relative momentum strategy

This is where the turnover of various shares of a certain asset class is compared with the other. Investors will generally favor buying strong performance securities and selling weak performing securities.

Swing Trading
Swing Trading is a strategy that focuses on short-term trends in taking smaller gains and cutting losses faster. The profits can be smaller but may accumulate into outstanding annual returns when achieved continuously over time. Swing trading positions are usually held for a few days to a few weeks but may last longer. The swing trader's emphasis is not on returns that grow over weeks or months; a trade's typical period is something like 5 to 10 days. You can make many small wins in this way, which will add up to great overall returns. If you're satisfied with a gain of 20 percent for a month or more, increases of 5 or 10 percent per week or two will add up to substantial earnings.
Position Trading
Position trading is a traditional trading technique where a person keeps a long-term position in a stock, usually for months or years. Position traders disregard short-term market movements in favor of taking advantage of longer-term patterns. Position trading encompasses the longest time frame of all trading strategies. Therefore, there is a larger benefit opportunity – as well as an enhanced intrinsic risk.

2.2 Trading Markets: Forex, Stocks and Options

There are different trading markets that people trade-in based on their preferences. These are Forex Markets, Stock Markets and Options Markets. We will now explain in detail these different trading markets.
Forex
The foreign exchange market, or Forex (F.X.), is a decentralized marketplace that facilitates the purchase and sale of different currencies. This is done via the interbank market over the counter (O.T.C.) rather than on a centralized exchange. There are several reasons why traders are drawn to Forex:

- The FX-market size

- A wide range of tradable currencies

- Various volatility levels

- High rate of sale

- Trading 24 hours a day, during the week

Unlike most economies, the foreign exchange market operates such that it is responsive to demand and availability. Using a very basic example, if European citizens holding Euros demand strong for the U.S. dollar, they will exchange their Euros for Dollars. The U.S. Dollar's value will rise while the Euro's value will fall. Keep in mind that this transaction only affects the currency pair EUR / USD and, for example, will not cause the USD to depreciate against the Japanese Yen.

Triggers in the Forex Market
The example above is just one of many factors that can shift the F.X. market. These involve large macroeconomic developments such as a new president's inauguration, or country-specific indicators such as the predominant interest rate, G.D.P., unemployment, inflation, and G.D.P. debt ratio, to list just a handful. Top traders use an economic calendar to keep up with these major economic announcements that may push the sector. What's so attractive in Forex? The foreign exchange sector allows major corporations, states, retail merchants and private entities to swap one currency for another and to take effect in the interbank (between banks) system. The benefit of getting Forex trading among global banks is that Forex can be traded around the clock (throughout the week). As the Asian trading session ends, European and U.K. banks, arrive online before handing over to the U.S. The entire trade day begins as the U.S. session moves into the next day's Asian session. What makes this sector much more appealing to some traders, according to BIS Triennial Survey 2016, it is the most competitive market in the world, having an estimated regular trading amount of 5.1\$ trillion. That means traders can quickly enter and exit positions because there are plenty of eager foreign exchange buyers and sellers.

Working of Forex Market
The principles behind Forex dealing are relatively straightforward. If you think a currency's value will (appreciate) go up, you'll buy the currency. This is classified as "slow-moving" You sell the currency because you fear the currency will go down (depreciate). This is regarded as "fast travel."

Forex Market participants
Within the foreign exchange market, there are two types of market participants. They are hedgers and speculators. Hedgers often aim to stop severe exchange-rate shifts. Think about big conglomerates like Shell and how they try to circumvent their vulnerability to fluctuations of foreign currencies. On the other hand, speculators are risk-seeking and

always looking for exchange-rate volatility to profit from. They trade at the major banks and supermarkets.

Learn to Read a Forex Quote

All traders need to understand how to read a Forex quote, as this will determine the price you are entering and exiting. Looking at the currency pool below, the first currency in the EUR / USD pair is regarded as the base currency, which is the Euro, whereas the second currency in that pair (USD) is defined as the variable or quote currency.

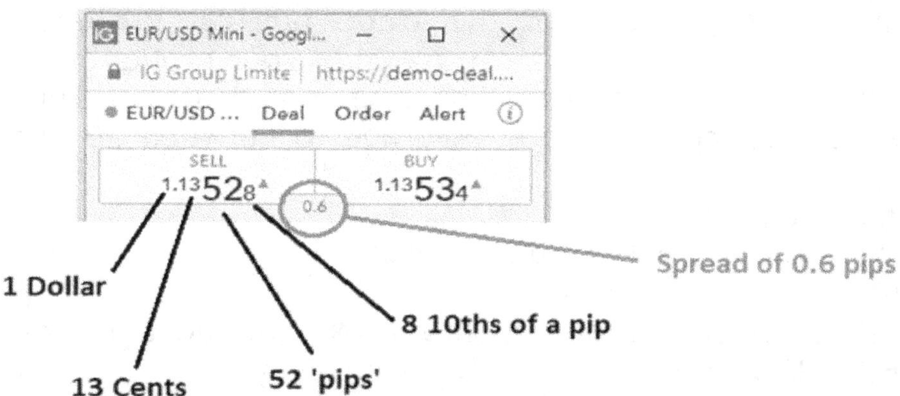

Prices are provided up to 5 decimal places for most F.X. markets, but the first four are the most significant. The number to the left of the decimal point means that the vector currency is one unit. It is the USD in this example and is, therefore, $1. The following two digits are the cents; that's 13 U.S. cents in this case. The third and fourth digits are fractions of one cent, which are called pips. It is important to note that the number is known as a 'pip' in the fourth decimal place. If the E.U.R. depreciate by 100 pips against the USD, the current sale price represents the lower price of 1.12528 because it would cost less in USD to purchase 1 Euro.

Reasons for Trading Forex

Trading Forex has many advantages over other markets, as explained below:

Low Transaction Costs

Forex traders usually make their profits out of the spread if the deal is opened and closed before any overnight funding fees are added. Forex trading stands thus cost-effective once measured counter to a market such as equities that attracts commission fees.

Low Spreads

Ask/Bid spreads are relatively small owing to the availability of big F.X. pairs. The spread is the main obstacle when dealing and needs to be resolved as the price swings in your favor. Any additional pips going in your favorite is a pure benefit.

More Profitable Opportunities

Forex trading allows traders to take speculative positions on upward (value-appreciating) and downward (value-depreciating) currencies. Additionally, many different Forex pairs are available for traders to spot profitable trades.

Leverage Trading

Forex trading involves utilizing leverage. This implies a trader will not have to pay the whole cost of the trade but can instead bring a percentage of the cost down. This can magnify your profits but also your losses. We propose a structured Risk Analysis strategy. This can be accomplished by reducing the total leverage to between 10 and one or fewer.

Forex Trading Lingo

Listed below are the key Forex trading jargons:

Base Currency

This is the first currency that appears when quoting a currency pair. Looking at EUR/USD, the Euro is the base currency.

Variable/Quote Currency

This is the second currency in the quoted currency pair and is the U.S. Dollar in the EUR/USD example.

Bid

The bid price is the highest price that a purchaser (the bidder) is prepared to pay. When you are searching to sell a Forex pair, this is the price you will notice, usually to the left of the quote. It is usually in red.

Ask

This is the opposite of the bid and indicates the lowest price a seller agrees to accept. When you are looking to buy a currency pair, this is the price you notice and is often to the right. It is usually in blue.

Spread

The disparity between the bid and the asking price is the real spread on the underlying Forex market plus the broker's added spread.

Pips/Points

A pip or point corresponds to a step in the 4th decimal position by one digit. This is also how traders respond to currency pair moves, i.e., Today, GBP / USD has raked 100 pips.

Margin

This is the amount of money that is necessary to open a leveraged position. Margin is the difference between the total value of your position and the funds that the broker lends to you.

Margin call

The margin call is triggered when the overall invested capital falls below a defined amount after adding or deducting gains or losses. Traders are then called for the replenishment of margins.

Liquidity

A currency pair is called liquid because it can be quickly acquired and exchanged since other parties participate in the currency pair.

Spot Forex

This form of Forex trading involves the purchase and sale of real money. You can buy a certain amount of pound sterling, for example, and exchange it for euros. If the pound's value is boosted, you will swap the euros for pounds again, earning more money than you used to spend on the purchase.

Long trade

If you acquire a currency, you will be conducting a long trade hoping the value will rise and profit from the disparity between the purchase price and the selling price.

Short trade

You are selling a currency intending to benefit from its current price, so you will buy it back at a lower value, gaining from the difference.

Stocks

Stocks are a form of investment in a company and a share in its profits. Investors purchase stocks to profit from their investment. Simply put, stocks are a method of accumulating wealth. You own a share of the company that issued the stock when you invest in it. Ordinary people invest in some of the world's most successful companies through stocks. Stocks are a way for businesses to raise capital.

Reason for owning stocks

When you buy a company's stock, you're effectively purchasing a partial right to the company's ownership. Is that a guarantee that you'll be seated next to Tim Cook at Apple's next shareholder meeting? No, it's not true. However, in most cases, it does imply that you have the right to vote at those meetings if you choose to do so. However, the primary motivation for stock ownership is to generate a profit. The return can result from the following two options:

- The stock's price rises. If you want, you can then sell the stock for a profit.

- Dividends are paid on the stock. Although not all stocks pay dividends, many of them do. Dividends are payments made to shareholders from a company's earnings, and they're usually made quarterly.

It is recommended to buy stock not only in one company. You must diversify your portfolio that contains stocks in many companies.
Stock Market
The word "stock market" is most used to refer to 1 of the main stock market indexes, like S& P 500 or Industrial Average of Dow Jones. Because it's difficult to keep track of every single stock, these indexes focus on a subset of the market, and their performance is regarded as representative of the entire market. You might see a news headline stating that the stock market has dropped or that the stock market has risen. Typically, this means stock market indexes have risen or fallen, implying that the stocks within the index have gained or lost value. Those who buy and sell stocks hope to profit from the fluctuation in stock prices.

Trading in Stocks
When you're ready to invest in stocks or mutual funds, you'll typically do so through the stock market, which anyone with a brokerage account can access. To invest in the stock market, you don't have to be an official "investor"; for the most part, anyone can do so. And once you've made your first investment, you'll be joining the ranks of investors all over the world who use the stock market to build long-term wealth. But first, you must understand what the stock market is, how it operates, and a few basic investment strategies.

Working of Stock Market
The stock market comprises a network of exchanges, including the New York Stock Exchange and the Nasdaq. An initial public offering, or I.P.O., is when a company sells shares of its stock on a stock exchange. Investors purchase these shares, allowing the company to raise funds to expand its operations. The exchange then tracks the supply & demand of each listed stock, allowing investors to buy and sell these stocks among themselves. The amount of every security, or the levels at which stock market participants — investors and traders — are willing to buy or sell, is influenced by supply & demand. Buyers submit a maximum amount or

a "bid" they are ready to pay, which is usually less than what sellers "demand" for in trade. The bid-ask spread is the name for this difference. A buyer must raise his price, or a seller must lower hers for a trade. When buying stock, you'll see the bid, ask, and bid-ask spread on your broker's website, but the difference in most cases will be pennies so that it won't be a big deal for beginners and long-term investors.

Know-How to Invest in Stock Market

Individual stocks can be purchased using a brokerage account or an individual retirement account (I.R.A.). You can open both accounts with an online broker and use them to buy and sell investments. The broker serves as an intermediary between you and the stock exchanges. Online brokerages have simplified the signup process, and once you've funded your account, you can choose the right investments for you. There are risks associated with any investment. On the other hand, stocks carry higher risk — and a higher potential reward — than other investments.

Options

A derivative is a contract that gives the buyer the right, but not the obligation, to buy or sell the underlying asset at a specified price by a certain date (expiration date) (strike price). Calls and puts are the two types of options. Options in the American style can be exercised at any time before they expire. Only on the expiration date can European-style options be exercised. Options and options trading is explained in detail in the ensuing chapter.

2.3 Difference Between Forex, Stocks and Options

Explained below are the key differences between the different markets based on their features:

24 Hours trading

Compared to Options and Stocks trading, one advantage of the Forex Exchange Trading Systems (Forex) is the capability to trade twenty-four hours a day, five days a week if desired. The Forex market is open for the longest period of any market. It's great to have unlimited time each week to make trades if your goal is to make double-digit gains in a market. When a major event occurs worldwide, you can be among the first to profit from the situation by using Forex Trading. You won't have to wait for a market to open in the morning, as you would with Options or Stocks. You can trade at any time of day or night from the comfort of your computer.

Trade Execution

You get immediate trade executions when you use the Forex Currency Trading System. There is no lag, as there can be in Options, Stocks, or other markets. And instead of guessing which price your order will be filled at, your order will be filled at the best possible price. Your order will not "slip" as it might with Options. There is a lot more liquidity in Forex Trading than in Options Trading to help with "slippage."

Liquidity

Like Stocks and Options Trading, Forex Trading has the advantage of being more liquid than any other market. There is no comparison with the Forex Market, which has an average daily volume of close to 2 trillion dollars. Foreign currency trading (Forex) has far more liquidity than the stock and options markets. This means that Forex traders will be much easier to fill than Options trades when trading. This increased speed equates to a higher potential profit. When you combine this with Forex Trading's instantaneous trade execution, you can quickly make many trades.

Commissions

Because Forex or F.X. trading is an interbank market that matches buyers and sellers in real-time, there are no commissions. Unlike other markets, there are no middleman brokerage fees. There is a spread among the ask prices & bid, wherever Forex trading organizations make a little of their money. This means that when you trade Forex, you may save money compared to stock and options trading, where commissions are charged because you are dealing with a brokerage firm.

Greater Leverage

Compared to stock and options trading, online forex trading can provide you with a lot more leverage. On the other hand, options allow you to manage putt and call options so that you greatly increase your leverage. When you know what a currency is going to do, leverage can be very useful. When it comes to Forex, you can make a lot more money if you make the right move.

Limited Risk

Because Forex traders should set limits on their positions, the probability is limited because the online competencies of Forex Trading systems inevitably initiate the margin call when the margin amount exceeds the account value in dollars. This prevents any Forex trader from losing a huge amount of money if the market turns against them. It's an excellent safety feature that isn't always present in some other financial markets. In addition, Forex differs from Options in that you only have a limited amount of time to trade before the options expire.

CHAPTER 3: What is Options trading?

The Chicago Board Options Exchange has defined options as:
The option is some contract that gives the buyer the right, but never the obligation, to buy or sell an underlying asset (such as an index or stock) at a certain price on & before the specific date. Like a bond, an option is an option

That definition could just be written in ancient Greek for most casual investors. On the other hand, brokers occasionally buy and sell options for investors who have no idea what they are, can't appreciate or afford the risk, and may not even be aware that the transactions are taking place. Contracts that give the owner the right to sell or buy an asset at a set price for a set period are known as options. Depending on the type of options contract, the said period could be as brief as a day or as lengthy as a couple of years. Trading options are easy to grasp once you've mastered a few key concepts. Multiple asset classes are commonly used in investor portfolios. Stocks, bonds, ETFs, and even mutual funds are examples of these. When used correctly, options are another asset class that provides many benefits that trading stocks and ETFs alone cannot.

Options are traded on a variety of underlying assets. Options can be used in various ways, including to speculate or mitigate risk, and they can be traded on a variety of underlying securities. Equities, indexes, and exchange-traded funds (ETFs) are the most popular underlying securities (Exchange Traded Funds). There are several distinctions between index-based options and those based on equities as well as ETFs. Before you begin trading, it's critical to understand the differences. Trading options is all about taking calculated risks. If statistics and probability are your greatest strengths, volatility and trading options are likely to be as well.

3.1 What Is Options Trading?

Options trading is simply the act of trading options on securities traded on the stock or bond markets (along with ETFs and the like). To begin, you must use a brokerage to buy or sell options. The strike price of a call option for a stock, for instance, will be decided based on the stock's current price when purchased. For example, if a stock's share price is $1,540, any strike price (the price of a call option) that is higher than that stock's share price is considered "out of the money." In contrast, if the strike price is less than the current stock price, it is said to be "in the money." The opposite is true for put options (right to sell): strike prices that are below the current share price are considered "out of the money," and vice versa.

What's more, any "out of the money" options- whether call or put- will be worthless when they expire (this means that you need to have an "in the money" option while trading on the stock market). Call options are usually bullish, whereas put options are normally bearish. Fridays are when most options expire, but there are some exceptions (for instance, monthly, bi-monthly, quarterly, etc.). Six-month contracts are common in option contracts.

3.2 Historical and Implied Volatility

You only need to worry about two types of volatility as an individual trader: historical volatility and implied volatility. In options trading, volatility refers to the magnitude of a stock's price swings. As you might expect, high volatility in securities (such as stocks) equates to higher risk, while low volatility equates to lower risk. Stocks with high volatility (those whose share prices fluctuate a lot) are more expensive when trading options on the stock market than those with low volatility.

However, owing to the erratic nature of the stock market, even low volatility stocks could become high volatility ones ultimately).

3.2.1 <u>**Options and Historical Volatility**</u>

Historical volatility depicts how much the stock price fluctuates daily over one year in the past. Because it quantifies how much a stock fluctuates daily over one-year, historical volatility is an excellent measure of volatility. On the other hand, implied volatility assesses a stock's (or security's) future volatility depending on the market during the option contract's life.

3.2.2 <u>**Options and Implied Volatility**</u>

Implied volatility is incumbent on what the market is implying the stock's volatility would be in the future, over the option contract's life. One of the most key concepts for options traders to grasp is implied volatility, which can help you decide the probability of a stock reaching a particular price by a certain date. It can also be used to predict how volatile the market will be in the future.

3.5 Types of Options

There are only two types of options available: "put" and "call." These are commonly referred to as "puts" and "calls." You can buy or sell as many option contracts as you want, but each contract handles 100 shares of stock. It's important to note that the owner of either a call or a put option contract is under no obligation to exercise her or his right to buy or sell.

3.5.1 Call Options

A call option contract gives the holder the right to buy 100 shares of a specific security at a specific price and within a certain time frame. When you buy a call option, you're buying the right to buy 100 shares of a specific stock from the option's seller at a predetermined price, known as the "strike price." If you don't use the call by a particular date, it will expire. To buy a call option, you must pay a fee to the call's seller, known as a "premium." When you buy a call option, you're hoping that the stock's market price that you're buying will rise shortly. What is the reason for this? If the stock price rises above the strike price, you could indeed exercise the call and buy the stock from the call's seller at the strike price or a price lower than the stock market value. Then you have the option of keeping the shares (which you got for a good price) or selling them for a profit. But what occurs if the stock price falls instead of rising? Your loss is restricted to the cost of the premium because you let the call option expire.

3.5.2 Put Options

A put option contract gives the holder the right to sell 100 shares of a specific security at a certain price within a certain time frame. When you purchase a put option, you are purchasing the right to compel the person who sells you the put to buy 100 shares of a specific stock from you at the strike price. You want the stock price to fall below the strike price when you hold put options. If it does, the put seller will be obligated to purchase shares from you at the strike price. The said strike price would be higher than the current market price. A put option resembles the insurance policy in contradiction of the shares losing much value because you can force the option seller to purchase your shares at a price above market value. If the market price rises rather than falls, your shares will appreciate, and you can easily let the option expire, as you will only lose the premium you paid for the put.

3.6 Selling and Buying a Put Option

You can produce double-digit income & returns by selling put options even in an overvalued, flat, or bearish market. For big returns on investment, you do not require quick business growth or any solid bull market. In the case of a market collapse, you may even grant your investments a 10 percent guarantee against the downside. In other words, if the market falls by 25%, your equity positions are likely to fall by only 15%. You can also enter stock positions exactly at the price you want and keep the cost base low. You should try to purchase in a declining market to get a greater bargain instead of buying at presently available market rates. There is a perfect period and place for selling put options like any device, and at certain times it is not an optimal strategy. This is a sophisticated and best way of entering equity positions when used correctly.

To option sellers, the two most critical things are the strike and the bid. The strike is the amount you agree to buy the shares for if the option is exercised, and the bid is about the amount you can expect to earn on selling the option. If you sell an option with a strike price of $30 below the current stock price of $30.50, you will now receive $143 from the option buyer, and you will be obliged to purchase 100 shares of the company at $30 each if the buyer wishes, for a total of $3,000, at any time before the option expires in 3.5 months.

Suppose the company's stock generally stays above $30 / share over the next 3.5 months. In that case, the option buyer probably won't assign the shares to you, as there would be no reason for her to force you to pay exactly $30 / share when the market price is already above $30 / share. Her option will expire worthlessly, you will keep your $143 premium, and your $3,000 in secured cash will be released for another option to be sold. Here is the calculated rate of return, if the right expires: $143 / $2,857 = 0.05 = 5%

After around 3.5 months, you made a return yield of 5 percent on your initial currency. This will be around 18 percent annualized returns on your investment if you practice that for the remainder of the year a few times. Compare this with the historical return of the S&P 500 of around 9%. Compared to average stock returns, you're being charged a huge amount of money to only hang around and wait for a market drop on a business you'd like to buy. On the contrary, if the stock dips to $29.50 / share, you still must retain the $143 premium, and the buyer option will assign you to purchase the 100 shares for $30 each.

This means that your effective cost base for buying those shares was only $28.57, which, as you wanted, is below your target buy price. You ended up having to purchase them for $30 apiece, but you still got a $1.43 / share bonus upfront, which covered some of the expense. The total cost structure is that for 100 securities, you must spend $28.57 / share, or $2.857. So instead, you hold 100 shares of a company already selling for $29.50 each. You purchased a wonderful business at a decent price, and ideally, you should still anticipate lots of growth in profits and dividends over time.

3.7 Basics of Option Contracts

Let us understand the salient of call and options contracts and trading mechanisms.

3.8 Salient of Call Option

The following components contain the major characteristics of an option:
Strike Price
When a derivative contract is exercised, the strike price is the price to be bought or sold. The strike price for call options is the price at which the option holder can purchase the security; the strike price for put options is the price at which the security could be sold. The exercise price is another name for the strike price. The strike price of put and call options is an important factor to consider. A stock option call, for example, gives the buyer the right but not the obligation to purchase the stock at the strike price in the future.
Similarly, a stock option put buyer has the right but not the obligation to sell the stock at the strike price in the future. The most significant aspect of the option value is the strike or exercise price. When a contract is first written, strike prices are established. It informs the investor of the price at which the fundamental asset should trade for the option to be into money (ITM). Strike values are standardized, which means they are set at specific dollar amounts, such as $41, $42, $43, $102, $105, and so on. The value of an option is determined by the price gap between the underlying stock price and the strike price. If the strike price of a call option is higher than the underlying stock price, the option is out of the money for the buyer (OTM). The option may still have value based on volatility and time until expiration in this case. This is because that these two factors can put the option in the money in the future. If an underlying stock value is higher than the strike price, an option would possess intrinsic value & will also be profitable. When the underlying stock price is under the strike price, the purchaser of the put option is in the money, and when the underlying stock price is over the strike price, the buyer is out of the money. An OTM option will not possess intrinsic value; however, it might have value depending on the underlying asset's volatility and the remaining time until expiration.
Premium
The cost of the option, for either the buyer or the seller
Expiration

When the option runs out and is settled

3.9 Salient of Put Option

A put option contract gives the owner the right to sell security within a given time frame within a given time frame . Each contract represents 100 share or the stock on which the option is based. Putting options enables traders to magnify downward market changes, transforming a slight price decline into a big benefit for the put buyer.

Trading Calls and Puts

Buying stock provides a long position for you. Buying a call option will give you a potentially long position in the underlying stock. Short selling stock provides you with a short position. Selling a naked or uncovered call in the underlying stock gives you a potential short position. Buying a put option in the underlying stock gives you a potentially short position. Selling a put option gives you a theoretically long place in the stock underlying it. Those who purchase options are classified as investors, and others who offer options are named options writers. Here's the big difference between holders and writers. There is no requirement to call investors and put investors (buyers) to buy or sell. They are granted the opportunity to exercise their privileges. This reduces the chance of options owners just paying the premium. However, call writers and put writers (sellers) are obliged to buy or sell if the option expires. This means a seller may need to make good on a purchase or sell pledge. It also means that sellers of options are subject to additional, infinite threats in certain situations. It ensures writers will risk a lot more than the quality of premium options.

Buying a call option is betting that the price of a share of security (such as a stock or index) will rise over a set period. If you purchase a call option for Alphabet (AOOG) at $1,500 and are bullish on the stock, you forecast that the stock's price will rise. When you buy put options, you're betting that the underlying security's price will fall over time (so you're pessimistic about the stock). For example, if you buy a put option on the S&P 500 at $1,800 per share, you are bearish on the stock market and believe the S&P 500 will fall in value over time (perhaps to $1,500). Because you bought the put option when the index was at $1,800 per share (supposing the strike price was at or near that level), you'd be able to sell it for the same price (not the new, lower price). The price of the underlying security, the time until the option expires, and the volatility of the underlying security all influence option trading (especially in the stock market). The option's premium (price) is determined by the option's intrinsic value and its time value (extrinsic value).

3.10 Time Value and In the Money, At the Money and Out of the Money

In the Money
Let us understand the concepts related to options' time value, in the money, at the money and out of the money.
In the Money
If you buy an option that is already "in the money" (indicating it will profit right away), the premium will be higher because you will be able to sell it right away for a profit. In the case of call options, contracts that are "in the money" are those with an underlying asset price (ETF, stock, etc.) then strike price. If the put option's strike price is less than the current price of the underlying asset, the contract will be "in the money" (stock, ETF, etc.)
At the Money
If you have an option that is "at the money," on the other hand, the option is equal to the current stock price. And, as you might expect, an option that is "out of the money" will have no added value since it is currently not profitable.
Out of the Money
You can sell options to collect a time premium if an option (whether a put or call option) proceeds to be "out of the money" around its expiration date.
Time Value in Options
The time value, also known as the extrinsic value, is the value of an option greater than its intrinsic value-or, above the "in the money" area. The more time an option has before it expires, the more time it must make a profit, so its premium (price) will be higher due to its higher time value. In contrast, the less time an options contract has until it expires, the lower its time value. This is because the less additional time value would be added to the premium). In other words, the more time an option has before expiration, the more time value would be added to the premium (price), and the less time it has before actual expiration, the less time value would be added to the premium (price).

3.11 In options trading, the Option traders borrow from the Greeks

Options traders use the Greek Alphabet to refer to how option prices are anticipated to change in the market. This is crucial to trading success. Gamma, Delta, and Theta are the most referenced. The values are theoretical, but they would help describe the key factors driving movement in option pricing and collectively suggest how the marketplace expects an option's price to change. There never is a 100% assurance that these predictions will be accurate to put it another way.

3.12 Option trading starts with your financial goals

Like many experienced traders, Options traders have a good understanding of the financial goals and optimal market position. The way you approach and think about money, in general, will influence how you trade options. Before you finance your account and begin trading, the greatest thing you could do is define your investment objectives.

3.13 Option traders speak their lingo

You can sell a put or buy a call when trading options. You can be tall or short, and your height has nothing to do with it. As a result, you can be in-the-money, at-the-money, or out-of-the-money. In a room full of option traders, those are just a few of the popular words you'll hear.

3.14 Pros and Cons

One of the most appealing aspects of options trading is its purported safety. Options are often more resilient to market price changes (and downturns), could really help increase income on present and future investments, will often get you better deals on a variety of equities, and, maybe most importantly, could even help you capitalize on that equity rising or falling over time without having to invest in it directly, according to Nasdaq's options trading tips. Trading options, of course, have drawbacks, one of which is a risk. Risks involved with options trading can be interpreted in various ways, but they mainly revolve around the market's volatility or uncertainty. Expensive options, for example, have a high level of uncertainty, implying that the market for that asset is volatile and trading it is risky.

3.15 Striking Characteristics of Options

Options, like other types of assets, can be purchased through a brokerage account. Options are powerful because they can help an individual's portfolio. They do so by providing additional income, protection, and even leverage. Depending on the situation, there is usually a scenario of options tailored to an investor's target. A popular example of limiting downside losses is to use options as a beneficial hedge against a falling stock market. Options could also be used to produce recurring income.
Furthermore, they are frequently used for gambling purposes, such as betting on stock direction. Options trading entails certain risks, which the investor should be aware of before making a trade. Options come with risks and are therefore not suitable for everyone. Option trading is inherently risky and carries a high risk of failure.

- The option is some contract that gives the purchaser the right but not the obligation- to sell or buy an underlying resource at a specified price on or before a certain date.

- Options are also known as derivatives because they derive value from the underlying assets. • Traders use income, speculation, and risk-hedging options.

- While a stock option contract usually contains 100 percent of the underlying stock, options can be written on various underlying properties, including debt, currency, and product.

Options Provide a Hedge Against Losses
Purchasing options can provide a hedge against losses, and they can be used prudently in this regard. However, numerous options strategies are little more than gambling and therefore can significantly increase your risk. The sale of "uncovered" calls is a simple example. Remember that when exercising a call, the seller of the call must deliver stock. If you sell a call on a stock, you already have, the call is "covered" by those shares, and you've already paid for it. You'll simply deliver the shares to the option holder if the option is exercised. However, if you sell an

"uncovered" call, which means you don't yet own the stock, your loss potential is limitless. If you exercise your option, you'll have to purchase the shares on the open market to meet your obligation, regardless of how high the price is at the time. If the share price has risen sharply due to a strong market upside movement or a significant announcement by the issuer, your losses could be massive.

3.16 Drawbacks of Options Trading

Given below are some of the disadvantages of options trading that must be considered, especially by beginners.

Options Expose Sellers to Extreme Losses

Contrary to an option buyer (or holder)-losses of much greater value- than the contract's price- can be incurred by the option seller (writer). Remember, when an investor opts to write a put or call at a predetermined price, he or she is required to purchase or sell shares within the time frame irrespective of whether the price is in his favor or against.

Options Are Time-Specific

Short term is the basic essence of options. Investors of options seek to benefit from a near-term market change that could take place for the trade/contract to generate payoff within days, weeks, or months. This requires two correct decisions: determining the best time to obtain the option contract and determining specifically whether to exercise, sell or step away before the offer expires. There isn't a deadline for long-term equity buyers. They have time to let their investment play out for years, even decades.

Pre-Requisites for Potential Traders

You must apply for clearance from your broker before even starting trading options. The broker may grant you a trading class that determines what kinds of options trades you are permitted to place after addressing several questions regarding your financial capital, investing background and your knowledge on the inherent risks of trading options. Any trader who is into options trading must hold in their trading account a minimum of $2,000, which is an industry-standard and a cost of investment worth contemplating.

Options' Trading Involves Additional Costs

Any trading strategy for options (such as selling call options on stocks you don't own) enables buyers to set up a margin account, which is simply a line of credit that acts as collateral if the transaction shifts against the investor. For the opening of a margin account, each brokerage company has various minimum conditions and may base the sum and interest rate on how much cash and shares are in the account. Usually, margin loan interest rates may range between the low single digits and the low double digits. If an investor is unwilling to make good on loan (or if the value of the trading account falls below a certain amount, which may happen due to regular market fluctuations), if he or she does not add more cash or securities to it, the lender may trigger a margin call and liquidate an investor's portfolio. The Options Clearing Corporation offers a comprehensive overview of the features and risks of standardized options and an overview of the U.S. federal income tax rules that impact those looking to invest in options and other financial products.

Bottom line

You must recognize the company's market inside out and determine whether to purchase, sell or retain stock for the long term and have a good understanding of the way the asset is going. Investors of options ought to be hyper-aware of those items and more. Success in options demands from investors to have a clear idea of the inherent value of the firm, but perhaps most significantly, they will need to have a sound thesis of how the business has been and would be impacted by short-term variables such as internal activities, sector/competition, and macroeconomic impacts. Many investors may conclude that options expose their financial lives to an excessive amount of risk. However, if you are interested in exploring the possibilities that options offer and have the discipline and capital to withstand potential losses, the options trading strategies for beginners can help limit your downside. Many options strategies are extremely complicated and risky. As a result, not all options strategies are appropriate for all investors. Writing puts or uncovered calls would be unsuitable for almost everyone, except for sophisticated, high-net-worth individuals who can afford and are willing to incur significant losses. Nonetheless, brokers occasionally engage in inappropriate options trading on behalf of customers who do not understand the risks. The next chapter is dedicated to various strategies that can be applied successfully for making money in trading options.

CHAPTER 4: Trading Strategy for New Options Traders

When you trade options, the contracts usually take the following form: The stock ticker (the name of the stock), the expiration date (typically in mm/dd/yy, though dates are sometimes flipped with the year first, month second, and day in the end), the call or put, strike price and the premium price (for instance, $4) are all listed on the contract. As an illustration of a call option for Apple stock, consider the following: APPL 01/15/2018 200 Call @ 4.

Regardless, the option trade would then look very different depending on which platform you are trading on. When trading options, you have various strategies to choose from, all of which differ in terms of risk, reward, and other factors. While there are dozens of strategies (the majority of which are complex), here are a few key ones that have been advised for beginners.

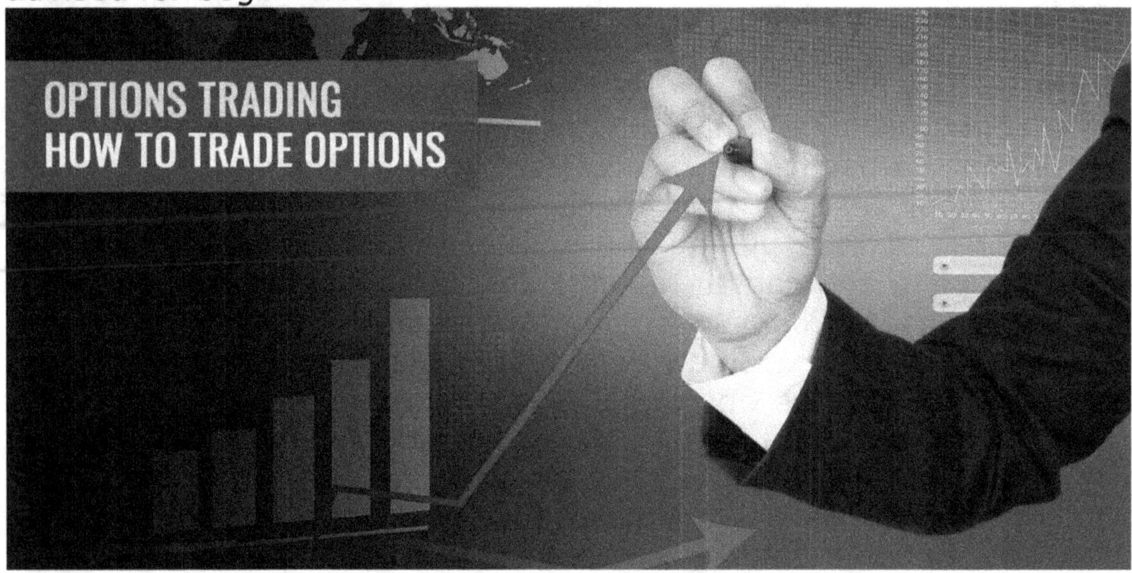

4.1 Straddles

When trading straddles (long in this case), you expect the asset (like stock) to be extremely volatile, but you don't know which way it will go (up or down). You buy a call and a put option at the same strike price, underlying price, and expiry date when using a straddle strategy. This strategy is commonly used when a trader expects a company's stock to decline or skyrocket in response to an event such as an earnings report.

When a company like Apple (AAPL) is preparing to release 3rd-quarter earnings on August 31st, an options trader can use a straddle strategy to buy a call option that expires on the date at the current Apple stock price, as well as a put option that expires on the same day at the same price.

4.2 Strangles

An investor will buy an "out of the money" call and an "out of the money" put for almost the same expiry date for almost the same underlying asset in a strangle (long in this example). Investors using this strategy believe the underlying asset (such as stock) will experience a significant price change, but they don't know how it will go. A long strangle is a relatively safe trade because the investor only requires the stock to move more than the total premium paid, regardless of which direction it moves. The advantage of a strangle strategy there is much less risk of loss because the premiums are lower because the options are "out of the money," which means they are less expensive to purchase.

4.3 Covered Call

A covered call is a good choice for you if you have long asset investments (such as stocks). This strategy is best for investors who are only slightly bullish or neutral on a stock. A covered call is created by purchasing 100 shares of regular stock and selling one call option/100 shares. This type of strategy can help you lower the risk of the current stock investments while also allowing you to profit from the option. When the stock price rises or remains relatively constant over the life of the option contract, covered calls could make you money. However, if the stock price falls too far, you could lose money on this trade. However, there is a probability of making money, provided it does take a little dip. However, by employing this strategy, you can protect your investment from share price declines while also allowing yourself to profit while the stock price remains stable.

4.4 Selling Iron Condors

The trader's risk can be conservative or risky based on their preference for this strategy. The trade's position for iron condors is non-directional, meaning the asset-like a stock- could go up or down, with profit potential over a wide range. To use this strategy, sell a put as well as buy another put at a lower strike price (basically a put spread), then combine it with buying a call as well as selling a call at a higher strike price (essentially a call spread) (a call spread). The puts and calls are short. You profit when the stock price remains between the two puts or calls (so even if the price fluctuates slightly, you profit). However, the strategy results in a loss when the stock price rises or falls dramatically above or below the spreads. As a result, the iron condor is thought to be in a market-neutral position.

4.5 Collars

A collar option technique, also known as a hedge wrapper or just collar, is an options strategy used to minimize an underlying asset's positive and negative returns. It restricts the portfolio's return to a defined range and may hedge the position against the underlying asset's potential volatility. The use of a protective put, and covered call option produces a collar position. It is produced more precisely by keeping an underlying stock, purchasing an option that is out of the money, and selling an option out of the money call.
How to create a Collar Position

The collar position is created by using the following method:

Collar Position=Long Underlying Asset + Long Put Option + Short Call Option

4.6 Combinations

A combination is an options trading strategy that entails purchasing and selling calls and putting options on the same underlying stock.

4.7 Call buying strategy

When you buy a call option, you get the right to buy the underlying futures contract at the strike price at any time before the contract expires. This happens infrequently, and there is little benefit in doing so. Most traders purchase call options since they assume a commodity market will rise, so they want to profit from it. You can also close the option before it expires, but only during market hours. You must first determine your goals before deciding on the best purchase option. When purchasing call options, keep the following in mind:

You must determine the time you plan to remain in the call option trade Many commodities and futures offer various options in terms of expiration months and strike prices, allowing you to choose an option that meets your needs. This will assist you in determining the amount of time required for a call option. You should buy a commodity with a minimum of two weeks remaining on it if you expect a commodity to finish its move higher within two weeks. If you only plan on being in the trade for a few weeks, you should avoid buying an option with six to nine months remaining because the options will be more expensive as well as you will lose some leverage. One thing to keep in mind is that option time premiums decay more quickly in the last 30 days. As a result, you could be correct in your trade assumptions, but the option loses much more time value, and you lose money. We recommend buying an option for 30 more days than you anticipate being in the trade.

Plan the Amount You Want to Invest in Buying A Call Option

Some options could be too expensive for you to purchase, or they may not be the right options at all, depending on the size of your account and your risk tolerances. Options would be more expensive in the money call than out of the money call. Also, the longer the call options are available, they'll cost. When you buy most options, in contrast to futures contracts, there is a margin. The entire option premium must be paid upfront. As a result, options in volatile markets such as crude oil can cost thousands of dollars. That may not be appropriate for all options traders, and you don't want to repeat the error of buying options that are far out of the money just because they are within your price range. The majority of deep out of the money options could well expire worthless, making them long shots.

Length of A Move You Expect from The Market

You must have an idea about the type of move you anticipate from the commodity or futures market to optimize your leverage and control your risk. Buying in the money options is usually the more conservative approach. Buying multiple contracts of out-of-the-money options is a more aggressive strategy. If the market makes a large move higher, out-of-the-money multiple options contracts will increase your returns. It's also riskier because you're more likely to lose your entire option premium if the market doesn't move.

Work out the breakeven point on buying call options

It is worked out as follows:

Strike Price + Option Premium Paid

This formula is used at option expiration because there is no time value left on the call options. If the options are deep in the money or far out of the money, you can sell the options at any time before expiration and keep the time premium.

Determine your stop-loss

For a short position, a call option can also be used as a low-risk stop-loss instrument. Stops for risk positions are recommended for traders and investors in volatile markets. A stop is a risk-reward function; you must never risk more on any investment than you intend to make. Stops have the drawback of causing the market to trade to a level that triggers a stop but then reverse. A long call option serves as stop-loss protection for those with short positions, but it can give you more time than a stop that closes the position when it reaches the risk level because the call option serves two purposes if the option has time left when the market becomes volatile.

- The call option would also act as price insurance for the short position, shielding it from further losses above the strike price.

- More importantly, the call option helps you to keep your position short even if the price rises above the insured level or strike price.

Markets frequently rise only to reverse course and plummet after stop orders are triggered. The call option will then keep a market participant in a short position if the option has time until expiration, allowing them to survive a volatile period before the market returns to a downtrend. A short position combined with a long call is primarily the same as a low risk long put position. Call options are instruments that can be used to take a direct position in a market to bet on the price rising or to safeguard an existing short position from a price rise.

4.8 Getting started with trading options

We have explained below in simple steps the process of starting trading options.

Open an options trading account

- You must first open an options trading account before you can begin trading options. Opening an options trading account necessitates a larger sum of money. Brokerage firms evaluate potential options traders based on their trading experience, risk awareness, and financial preparedness. The details will be recorded in an options trading agreement submitted to your prospective broker for approval. You'll need to provide the following details:

- Investment objectives

- Trading experience

- Personal financial information

- The types of options you want to trade

The broker will usually assign you an initial trading level based on your answers and the level of risk you are willing to take-typically 1 to 5, where 1 is the lowest risk, and 5 is the highest). This is how you'll be able to make certain types of options trades.

Pick which options to buy or sell
What type of options contract to take depends on which direction you anticipate the underlying stock to move?

- Buy a call option and sell a put option if you believe the stock price will rise.

- Sell a call option or a put option if you believe the stock price will remain stable.

- Buy a put option and sell a call option if you believe the stock price will fall.

Predict the option strike price
Purchasing an option is recommended if the stock price closes the options' expiration period "in the money. That is, the price must be below or above the strike price. You should purchase an option with a strike price that matches where you believe the stock will be during the option's lifetime. The premium, or the price you pay for an option, comprises two parts- time value and intrinsic value. If the stock price is above the strike, intrinsic value is the gap between the strike price and the share price. What's left is called time value, and it considers things like the stock's volatility, the time until expiration, as well as interest rates, in addition to other things.

Determine the option time frame

Every options contract has an expiration date that indicates when you could exercise the option. There are 2 types of options: American and European, which differ in terms of when they can be implemented. The American option might be applied at any time until expiration date, but European options could just be implemented on the day of expiration. Because American options give the option buyer more flexibility (and the option seller more risk), they are usually more expensive than the European counterparts. Expiration dates can be anything from a few days to a few months to a few years. Daily as well as weekly options are the riskiest and should only be used by experienced option traders. Monthly as well as yearly expiration dates are preferable for long-term investors. Longer expiration dates give the stock more time to move, as well as more time for the investment thesis to come to fruition. The longer the expiration period, the more expensive the option will be.

4.9 Trading Rules

Listed below are the trading rules both for the professional traders and the beginners:

- Divide the capital into some equal parts (if possible 10) & never risk higher than 1 share of the capital on a single trade.

- Trade just in stocks, options and currencies which are active and liquid

- Use the stop-losses

- Never over-trade and stick to guidelines regarding risk management

- Never let gains become losses

- Use trail stops to secure your money, and lock them

- Never trade in a rush

- Never get out of the market just because you've lost faith

- Don't guess where the tops and bottoms of the market are, but let the top and bottom of the market indicate

- Never average the losing trade

- Stop taking large losses and low gains

- Pay attention to risk factor

- Always trade within your capacities, financially and otherwise

- Never allow greed or fear to take hold of your winning positions

Avoid tips & rumors because people with vested interests spread these tips

4.10 Common Options Trading Mistakes

There are plenty of mistakes that can be committed even by the professional while trading options. These are:
- Selling for thrill & excitement

- High ego involved in trading.

- Risking money, you cannot afford to lose

- Too passionate about money

- Absence of trade system and lack of record-keeping

- Not allowing profits to run

- Allowing losses to increase

- Letting minor losses become major losses

- Not sticking to plans & strategies

- Anti-trend trading – short-selling on the bull market and going long on the bear market

4.11 Technical analysis for trading Options

In short-term trading, technical indicators enable the investor to recognize the trend and its trajectory. Since options are prone to time decay, the retention period takes on value. A stock trader can retain a position forever, while an options trader is constrained by the fixed time specified by the expiry date of the options. Due to time constraints, momentum indicators are common among options traders, which appear to identify overbought and oversold levels.

Relative Strength Index – R.S.I.

For options on specific securities, R.S.I. fits well. The strongest candidates for short-term trading dependent on R.S.I. are the options for extremely liquid, high-beta stocks.

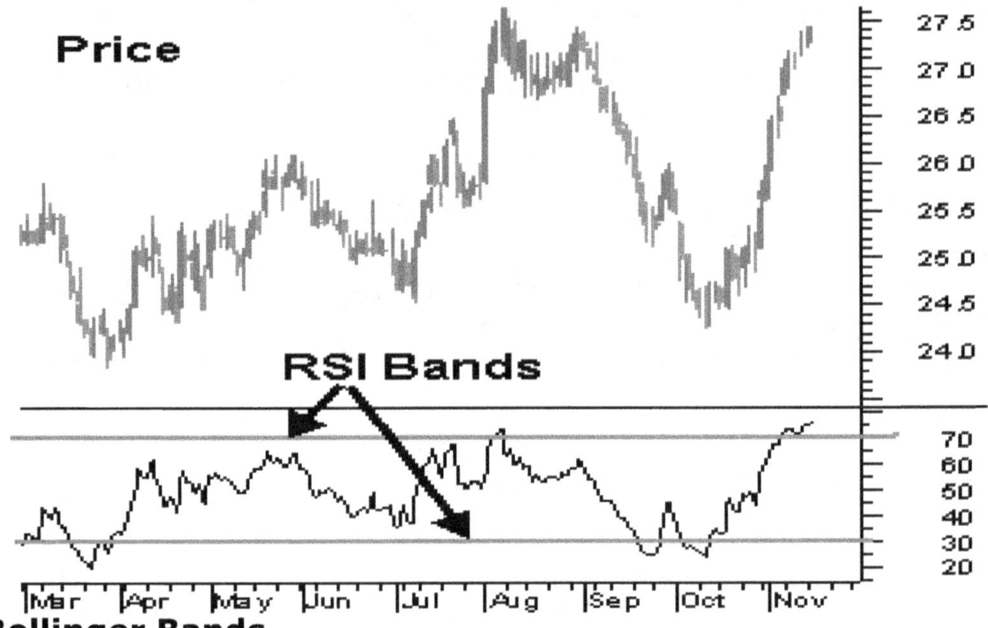

Bollinger Bands

The worth of volatility seems to be known to each options trader, & Bollinger band is amongst the most common approaches for calculating volatility. When volatility rises, the bands extend and contract when volatility declines. The more the price travels to the upper band, the more the security can be overbought, and the more the price rises to the lower band, the more it may be oversold. A shift of prices beyond the bands will indicate that the security is ripe for a turnaround, and traders of options should position themselves appropriately.

Intraday Momentum Index – I.M.I.

For high-frequency option traders seeking to gamble on intraday movements, an Intraday Momentum Index is a strong technical indicator. This incorporates the intraday candlesticks & R.S.I. principles, thereby providing the acceptable range to intraday trading (like R.S.I.) by suggesting degrees of overbought and oversold. Utilizing I.M.I., an options trader could be able to spot possible opportunities at an intraday correction to execute a bullish trade in an up-trending market or to execute a bearish trade at an intraday price bump in a down-trending market.

Money Flow Index – MFI

A momentum indicator that incorporates price and volume data is the Money Flow Index. It is often referred to as R.S.I. volume weighted. The

M.F.I. metric calculates the cash inflow and outflows into an asset over a specified period.

M.F.I. is best adapted for stock-based options trading (as opposed to index-based) and longer-duration trades due to reliance on volume data. This may be a leading sign of a trend transition as the M.F.I. moves in the same direction as the stock price.

Put-Call Ratio (PCR) Indicator

Using put options against call options, the put-call ratio calculates trading volume. Regardless of the actual put-call ratio's value, the shifts in its value signify a shift in general market sentiment.

The ratio is above 1 when there are more puts than calls, suggesting bearishness. The ratio is less than 1, suggesting bullishness, while call volume is greater than put volume. The put-call ratio, however, is often regarded by traders as a contrary measure.

Open Interest – O.I.

Open interest shows possibilities for open or unsettled contracts. O.I. does not generally imply a particular uptrend or downtrend, but it does include indicators of a given trend's intensity. Rising open interest implies fresh capital inflow and the current trend's longevity, while a slowing pattern implies a declining O.I.

Conclusion

Because options are a type of derivative, their value is determined by the underlying instrument's price. A stock can be the underlying instrument. However, other underlying instruments like an index, a currency, a commodity, or any other security could be. An option contract is a financial contract that gives an investor the option to sell or buy a specific asset at a predetermined price by a certain date. It does, however, include the right to purchase but not the obligation to do so. When it comes to an understanding the meaning of an option contract, it's important to remember that there are 2 parties involved: a buyer (also known as the holder) and a seller (also known as the writer). There are 2 types of options available. These are referred to as the call and put options. Contract size, premium or down payment, Strike price, Expiration date, Intrinsic value, Settlement of an option, and no obligation to buy or sell are all features of an option contract. Then, American options could be implemented until the expiration date, while European options might only be implemented. At the NSE, all index options appear as European options. Anyone interested in trading options should have a basic understanding of how options are priced. Several factors determine the options' value. The intrinsic value, current stock price, the time to expiration, the time value, and other factors such as volatility, interest rates, and so on are among them. Options have several advantages. These have a low cost of entry because, unlike stock transactions, they allow an investor and trader to take a position with a small sum of money. Another benefit of options is that they provide risk hedging. Options trading is also more flexible as compared to any other type of trading. Options work in all kinds of market conditions and are a valuable and profitable trading instrument.